Trial of the Rev. Edward Irving, M.A.
by Edward Irving

Address:
HardPress
8345 NW 66TH ST #2561
MIAMI FL 33166-2626
USA
Email: info@hardpress.net

7/6

TRIAL,

&c. &c.

TRIAL

OF THE

REV. EDWARD IRVING, M.A.

A

CENTO OF CRITICISM.

" I pr'ythee take the cork out of thy mouth, that I may drink thy tidings."

As You Like It.

𝕱𝔦𝔣𝔱𝔥 𝔈𝔡𝔦𝔱𝔦𝔬𝔫.

LONDON:

Printed by *Shackell and Arrowsmith, Johnson's-Court, Fleet-Street.*

PUBLISHED BY E. BRAIN,

BUTCHER-HALL-LANE, NEWGATE-STREET

MDCCCXXIII.

L'ENVOY TO SECOND EDITION.

BOARD OF CENSORS.

Wednesday, 11th Sept. 1823.

Mr. Chairman—Heyday !   What have we got here ?   " The Trial of the Rev. Edward Irving."

Examiner—A remarkably pleasant and amusing *jeu d' esprit* indeed, gentlemen.

Times—Very smart and clever I must own.

Courier—And very amusing.

Lit. Chron.—The speeches are much to the point.

Courier.—And the cross examination of the witnesses, most ingenious !

Examiner—Yes particularly happy. (*aside*) Yours especially, Mr. Courier.

a

Lit. Chron.—And the defence most eloquent and powerful.

Examiner—And the squibbery in the reporting department light and easy.

John Bull—A bit of foolery methinks, but withal, remarkably smart, and well done.

Times—Let me add too, as not its least praise ; so free from all malignity.

John Bull—Liberal egad ! (*aside*) Shown up to the life, and yet the first to praise.

Mr. Chairman—Well, gentlemen, you seem all to be pretty much agreed in opinion— I presume Mr. Secretary may enter it as the award of the Board——

Times—That it *deserves general circulation.*

Examiner—And forms a pleasant and useful pasquinade for those *who are anxious to have all sides of the question.*

Star—And is the only thing worth reading that has been written on the subject of Mr. Irving.

Mr. Chairman—Let judgment be entered up accordingly.

HIGH COURT OF COMMON SENSE.

SPECIAL JURY CASE.

TRINITY SESSIONS, 1823.

The KING, *at the Instance of* JACOB OLDSTYLE, *Clerk,* v. *the* REV. EDWARD IRVING, M. A.

FROM the extraordinary interest which this case excited, the doors of the Court were no sooner opened than it was filled in every part to excess, by an assemblage of persons of the first rank and distinction in the country. On the bench beside the Chief Justice, sat the Lord Chancellor and his brother Lord Stowell, Earl Liverpool, Earl Grey, Marquis of Lansdowne, Lord Erskine, Right Hon. Sir William Grant, Mr. Justice Bayley, Sir James Mackintosh, Mr. Canning, Mr. Peel, Mr. Huskisson, Mr. Tierney, Mr. Brougham ; and at the extremities of the bench, but railed off from the others (for in the Court of Common Sense it is not as in other Courts), the Duke of Somerset, Lord Kenyon, Sir Gerard Noel, Sir Harcourt

B

Lees, Mr. Peter Moore, Mr. Parkins, Romeo
Coates, and Dr. Dinwiddie. Earl Grosvenor was
put into a box by himself, and the prayer-book
placed out of his reach. The galleries were almost
entirely filled with elegantly dressed ladies, admitted by tickets from the Lady Patronesses at
Almack's. All its best blood was there. Among
a crowd of persons attending below the bench to
give evidence, were most of the active literary
characters about town connected with the periodical press ; and for reasons developed in the course
of the proceedings, it is necessary that we here
enumerate their names, as far as they were known
to us. We observed Dr. Stodart and Mr. Barnes
side by side ; Mr. Jerdan, Mr. Mudford, Mr. Haz-
litt, Mr. Cobbett, Lieut. Col. Torrens, Mr. Soane,
Sir Richard Phillips, Pierce Egan, Rev. Ingram
Cobbin, Rev. George Redford, Mr. Black, Dr.
Dreghorn, Mr. Thomas Campbell, Mr. Byerley,
Mr. Gifford, Mr. Haynes, Mr. Wooler, Mr. Coul-
ston, Mr. David Booth, Mr. D. W. Harvey, Rev.
Mr. Burder, Rev. Mr. Knox, Mr. Theod. Hook,
Paul Potter, Dr. Walsh, Mr. Robinson, Mr. Josiah
Conder, Mr. William Jones, Mr. Bell, Mr. Wal-
lace, Mr. Lamb, Mr. Gale Jones, Mr. R. Hunt,
and Mr. Moody (not the *Judy*.)

Mr. Serjeant Bishop appeared for the prosecution, along with whom were Mr. Parsons and Mr.
Macvicar.

The defendant conducted his own case, assisted
by Mr. Counsellor Phillips. Mr. Irving maintained
throughout a very firm and collected demeanour.

He seems to be about thirty-five years of age, and nearly six feet high. The general contour of his countenance is intellectual, though somewhat coarse, his complexion very dark, his hair black and bushy, whiskers tremendous. As one of his many critics has observed, " he would undoubtedly be a very handsome man," only he squints abominably.

The list of the special jurors being called over, the following gentlemen answered to their names: — ALDERMAN SIR JAMES SHAW, Bart., ALDERMAN BIRCH, ALDERMAN KEY, JAMES MILL, Esq., DR. ALEXANDER CROMBIE, A. STRAHAN, Esq., A. J. VALPY, Esq., HORACE TWISS, Esq. M. P.

The defendant having prayed a tales, the jury was completed by the following names from the common jury list. Mr. THOMAS UNDERWOOD, Mr. RICHARD TAYLOR, Mr. HURCOMBE, Mr. T. C. HANSARD.

CASE FOR THE PROSECUTION.

Mr. Macvicar opened the case to the jury. The present, he said, was a prosecution instituted at the instance of Mr. Jacob Oldstyle, Clerk, against the Rev. Edward Irving, Minister of the Caledonian Church or Chapel, in Cross Street, Hatton Garden. The indictment was laid on seven different counts.

First, For being ugly.

Second, For being a merry-andrew.

Third, For being a common quack.

Fourth, For being a common brawler.

Fifth, For being a common swearer.

Sixth, For being of very common understanding.

And, *Seventh,* For following divisive courses, subversive of the discipline of the order to which he belongs, and contrary to the principles of Christian fellowship and charity.

Mr. Serjeant Bishop, said, that he would not detain the court with any long harangue. He saw so many gentlemen of far higher talents than he could pretend to, so many lights of the age, in waiting, who would be called upon to state to the jury what they knew of the case, that it would be presumption in him to pre-occupy their minds with anything he could offer on the subject. He would state merely in vindication of his client, Mr. Jacob Oldstyle, that he had not instituted this prosecution from any feeling of personal resentment towards Mr. Irving, nor from any vain hope of gaining a name to himself, by measuring his strength with the great boar of the forest.—— He appeared here, not on his own account alone, but in the name and the behalf of the whole generation of the Oldstyles. He did not claim to be the best of the family, and therefore of right their Champion, but being the oldest among them, he had been called upon to stand forward and defend their common interests, from the rude assaults which Mr. Irving, in his ugliness and quackery, and divisive-mindedness, had made upon them. He loved his family, and could not refuse, though bending under a load of years, to make this humble effort, ere he died, to wipe off the stain attempted to be fixed on their name and reputation. The Learned Serjeant, said, that he would now proceed to call the witnesses who would prove the different charges, which his learned friend, Mr. Macvicar, had so clearly and explicitly laid before them. [Here some twenty voices from the body of the court cried out Stop! Stop! and a portly gentleman with spectacles, pushing forward to the Learned Serjeant, whispered something in his ear.]

Mr. Serjeant Bishop. "My Lord, it has been just intimated to me, that it will be an unpleasant circumstance to many gentlemen who are here to give evidence, and may withal be attended with dangerous consequences, if they are called by their individual names into the witness box. I need scarcely remind the court of the melancholy fate of Mr. Scott. The gentlemen are all in one way or another connected with different periodical works, and it is their wish, I understand, that each should be called by the name of the work to which he belongs. They have brought Masks with them, which, with the leave of the court, they will put on during examination."

Mr. Cobbett. "Not I, my Lord, thank God, I want no mask."

Mr. Wooler. "Nor I."

Dr. Dreghorn (aside). "Brazen faces need no masks."

Chief Justice. " It is a novel application, certainly. At common sense, however, we want no precedents to justify us in doing what seems right and proper. Let it be as the gentlemen please; each may mask or not, as he likes. It would be a shocking thing were any person to catch harm from his appearance here to-day, in aid of the ends of justice."

The Editor of the Times was then called, and examined by Mr. Parsons.

You are editor of The Times journal?—Yes.

It is the leading journal of Europe, is it not?—Undoubtedly.

How do you take the lead, Sir?

By guarding the candid and enlightened public against extravagant pretensions, wherever and whenever we meet them.

All sorts of pretensions?

No, Sir. I would beg leave to say, there is a fashion in every thing—in wigs and bonnets, in poetry and novel writing, and lastly, in actors and preachers. All this is matter of course; and while things go on in the ordinary way—while wigs do not accumulate their curls into perriwigs—nor bonnets swell into coal-scuttles—while our popular poets scribble only one poem, and our popular romancers only two novels a year—while our actors are content with one new reading in a play of Shakespeare; and our preachers aim at no praises beyond that of the regular frequenters of fashionable chapels; we, I say *we,*

Sir, are disposed to let things pass, and allow the "candid and enlightened public" to be pleased in their own way.

Do you know any thing of the defendant, Mr. Irving? Have you allowed *him* to pass?

Oh dear, no! The case is quite different with Mr. Irving. His popularity, Sir, absolutely frightened us, Sir, " from our propriety." When we learnt that statesmen and quack doctors, old ladies and judges, young ladies and students at law, all flocked with equal eagerness to hear this Caledonian orator : we became curious to know what could be the attractions to collect together such an heterogeneous mass.

And so you went to hear him preach?

Not only went to hear him preach, Sir, but read all that he had written.

Did you find out, then, what his attractions are?

After a serious consideration, I must profess, that we were utterly unable to discover. We were, in our own minds—(for we hate, Sir, to think with the minds of other people)—fully convinced that Mr. Irving is a man of very ordinary talents ; that his understanding is weak in its grasp, and limited in its observation ; and that his taste is of the very lowest order of badly-instructed school-boys.

You are aware that Mr. Irving was assistant to the celebrated Dr. Chalmers, of Glasgow : did it strike you, that he is of the same school?

Of the same school, Sir ! He is an imitator of the doctor's, indeed ; but no more like the prototype, than the inflated frog in the fable was like the bull he strove to resemble. For the energy of thought of the original, he gives us nothing but rumbling and distorted common-places ; for the impassioned and expressive diction of his master, we have nothing but antitheses without point, and epithets without distinctness ; while the poor and insignificant idea, wrapt up in a heap of tinsel and clumsy phraseology, looks like " the lady in the lobster," or a mouse under a canopy of state.

Give us, pray, a specimen of his quality.

" *Obey the Scriptures, or you perish.* You may despise the honour done you by the Majesty above ; you may spurn the sovereignty of Almighty God ; you may revolt from Creation's universal rule, to bow before its creator, and stand in momentary rebellion against its ordinances ;" and so forth. " But come at length it will, when revenge shall array herself to go forth, and anguish shall attend her, and from the wheels of their chariot ruin and dismay shall shoot far and wide among the enemies of the king, whose desolation shall not tarry, and whose destruction, as the wings of the whirlwind, shall be swift, hopeless as the conclusion of eternity, and the reversion of doom. Then around the fiery concave of the wasteful pit *the clang of grief shall ring*, and the *flinty heart*, which repelled tender mercy, *shall strike its fangs into its proper bosom ;*" and so on. All, all shall pass away ! And instead shall come the level lake that burneth, and the solitary dungeon, and the desolate bosom, and the throes and tossings of horror and hopelessness, and the worm that dieth not, and the fire that is not quenched. 'Tis written, 'tis written, 'tis sealed of heaven, and a few years shall reveal it all. Be assured, it is even so to happen to the despisers of holy writ : with this in arrear, what boots liberty, pleasure, enjoyment — all within the hour-glass of time, on the round earth's continent, all the sensibilities of life, all the powers of man, all the attractions of woman ! "

And this, you think, is the lady in a lobster ?

Yes. I would fearlessly ask, Sir, whether a boy at any public school would not have his exercise flung in his face—(a smile from Lord Grosvenor) —if he presented such trash to his master. We absolutely felt ashamed, and began to distrust our own judgment, when we found that we had one idea in common with such a turgid and shallow declaimer. Surely, surely (said we to ourselves), it cannot be long before this bubble bursts.

And all this you stated to the public ?—Yes.

Did you find that your exposure of the defendant's pretensions had the effect of putting an end to the public delusion ?

Quite the reverse. The crowds which thronged to the Caledonian chapel, instantly doubled. The scene which Cross-street, Hatton-garden, presented on the following Sunday, beggared all description. It was quite a Vanity Fair. Not one half of the assembled multitude could force their way into the *sanctum sanctorum*. Even we, ourselves, were shut out among the vulgar herd. For the entertainment of the excluded, however, there was Mr. Basil Montague, preaching peace and resignation from a window ; and the once celebrated Romeo Coates acting the part of trumpeter from the steps of the church, extolling Mr. Irving as the prodigy of prodigies, and abusing the Times for declaring that Mr. Irving was not " the god of their idolatry." We laughed heartily at the fool.

From what text did Mr. Romeo discourse ?

Proverbs vii. 7. " And behold, among the simple ones, I discovered a young man void of understanding"—(much laughter).

Did you on this, make any other attempt to bring back the public to reason ?

Yes, we did once more enter our protest in the name of good sense and common sense, against his fustian phraseology, his pigmy ideas, mounted on stilts, and all the other little tricks by which a mean understanding endeavours to acquire the character of depth and dignity of thought.

Cross-examined by MR. PHILLIPS.

Are you not, Sir, in the practice of inserting articles in your journal as from yourself, when they are, in fact, written by others ?—Yes, when *cleverly* written.

Is not Mr. Cobbett in the habit of supplying you with clever articles occasionally ?

Mr. Cobbett ! never, Sir : we should take shame

to ourselves if we polluted our pages with any thing from the pen of that arch mountebank and impostor.

But on your oath, Sir, did not Mr. Cobbett write those articles on the late Queen, which gained your paper so much of the bubble reputation?

A lie—an odious lie, upon my soul a d——d lie. (Accompanied with great violence of gesticulation.)

Keep your temper, Sir. Was it not so reported at least?

Yes. The old ruffian gave it out himself, that he had written them; but it was all a base and wicked invention of his own.

I must nevertheless ask you whether it was not this very same Mr. Cobbett who wrote the criticisms which you have repeated here to-day on Mr. Irving?

No, Sir; no earthly consideration could ever induce us to insert a syllable from the pen of that rascally grave-stealer, on any subject whatever.

Mr. Phillips. But Mr. Cobbett, your are perhaps aware, has done you the honour of agreeing with you in opinion as to the present case?

Honour, Sir! I know nothing about it; I am no reader of his trash.

And yet you quote him at times?

Yes, the blustering blockhead will start across our path now and then, when we like to stir him up with our long pole a little, for the diversion of the public. But he is so nauseous a dog, that when we have any thing to quote from him, we never defile our pens with the task, but toss him to the compositors, that they may print from his own detestable pages.

Admirable delicacy, indeed! Now, Sir, let me ask you, who have so freely condemned Mr. Irving as a man of *mean understanding*, whether you have not at the same time condemned Sir Walter Scott as a *writer of no imagination?*—Yes, I have.

And Lord Byron, as *destitute of all poetical talent?*—Yes.

Enough, Sir, you may go down.

I am *going down*, Sir.

The Editor of the Courier examined by Mr. Macvicar.

Mr. Macvicar (handing to the witness a copy of the Courier of Thursday, July 17, 1823). Is that a genuine copy of the Courier newspaper for Thursday, the 17th of July?—It is.

It contains, I see, an article on the subject of the controversy about Mr. Irving—is that your writing?—It is.

Had you heard Mr. Irving when you wrote it?

No; as there observed we had *not heard* the gentleman, and until we could do so without fighting our way into his church, we were resolved to remain contented with what we could hear of him.

You were enabled, however, to express an opinion of his merits?

Yes; from specimens which appeared in the Morning Chronicle (the only paper we read except our own) of what he had delivered in the pulpit, we were enabled to say, that he was the last preacher to whom we should choose to listen. What he uttered seemed to be a mere mass of gaudy, glittering words, without matter or method. What effect the mode of his delivery could have upon the tinsel of his language, we could not know, but we felt satisfied that if he could not reach the *minds* of his congregation, his influence on their *ears* and *eyes* would soon find its proper level.

Were these all your objections?

No. We were given to understand that he made the pulpit a theatre for coarse attacks upon individuals. Now we hold it to be the business of a clergyman simply to expound the word of God, to enforce the precepts of religion, and to animate his fellow Christians in the pursuit of moral duty. He is not to level his rebukes at persons, for what he may consider as an aberration from strict propriety of conduct; such a practice would convert a sacred place of worship into a hot-bed of angry passions and mutual animosities. Still less ought a preacher to fulminate *ex cathedrâ* petulant censures upon literary effusions.

What do you particularly allude to?

We had seen in the papers of the day some foolish, illiberal, and greatly misplaced remarks of his upon the Vision of Judgment, by our friend Southey, and its ribald parody, by Lord Byron. Do people, we asked, and again ask, go to church to hear trash like this?

Q. You concluded, I observe, with a prophecy?

Yes. I said then, and now I repeat, that by acts like these, and by a fustian Ossianic phraseology, Mr. Irving may for a time draw crowds, but I venture to predict, that unless he betakes himself to a sounder and purer method of pulpit oratory, the new church which there is a talk of building for him will not be wanted half so much as he will want a congregation.

Cross-examined by MR. PHILLIPS.

Look at that paper, Sir, and tell the Jury what it is.

It is a copy of the Courier of Monday, July 7.

Older by ten days than the Courier you have just been quoting ?—Yes.

You there give an account of Mr. Irving's preaching at Hatton Garden on the day preceding, as if you had been present ?—Yes.

You say the chapel was crowded to suffocation—that the heat was so intolerable that some stout-hearted men were absolutely fainting, and were obliged to be carried out of the crowd ; all which things you of course saw ?—Yes.

You describe Mr. Irving's person—his bushy hair—his large whiskers—his unfortunate squint ? Yes.

You say his prayers and his reading are very impressive, and that his sermon was a *masterpiece of oratory,* and *full of sound doctrine ?*—Yes.

And yet ten days after, you say you had *not heard* the gentleman, and that his sermons are *a mere mass of glittering, gaudy words, without matter or method?*—Yes.

I have nothing more to say to you, Sir. Good God! that by such witnesses as this my noble-minded client should be borne down and reviled!

Re-examined by Mr. Macvicar.

You can perhaps explain how this extraordinary discrepancy arises?

Quite easily, Sir. I have occasion to make frequent visits to Paris, and it was during one of these that the prior article, which Mr. Phillips rests so much upon, was written by an assistant, who, as my friend of *l' Etoile*, says, has got *un tete foible extremement*. (*Much laughter.*) Why, Sir, it was the same gentleman with the weak head, who sounded the famous retreat of the French behind the Ebro, while at the very moment I was at Paris, receiving instructions from the French ministers to do all I could to make the public believe that the game was all up with the Spaniards. He is constantly committing blunders of this sort.

Re-examined by Mr. Phillips.

On your oath, Sir, did not you find, on your return from Paris, a letter lying from your friend Southey, chiding you for praising to the skies in your journal, a man who had called his Vision of Judgment " a most nauseous and unformed abortion; vile, unprincipled, and unmeaning; a brazen-faced piece of political cant?"

Mr. Macvicar submitted, that Mr. Phillips was not at liberty to prove a written document by parole evidence. Notice should have been given to produce the letter.

Mr. Phillips declined pressing the question.

Mr. William Cobbett examined by MR. PARSONS.

Have you heard the defendant, Mr. Irving, preach?

I never go after fools, Sir.

Perhaps, Mr. Cobbett, you " keep a fool of your own," and then think yourself " wise?" *(A laugh.)*

Perhaps not, Mr. Jackanapes.

Come now, Cobbett, don't be angry; you are all on our side, you know; tell us, then, how you came to-know all about this Caledonian prodigy?

Why, I will tell you.——My friend William Hone, since he took to writing about Apocryphas and Mysteries, has become as pious and dreaming a noodle as any lank-haired fanatic in all England. It was only the other day he told me, that in making his famous defence on the three trials, which every body knows was a stammer and a halt all through, he verily thought he had the gift of tongues given unto him! The man is sadly gone. He can speak to you about nothing but the Maccabees, and Habbakuk, and Mahaleel, and Jeroboam, and Rehoboam, and goes moreover to church as regularly as my Lord Bexley, or that saintly gentleman, Mr. Butterworth. The God of his idolatry at present is Mr. Irving, *on whose ministry*, as the poor man calls it, he attends every Sabbath, with all his pretty little chubby children ; and it is from him I have heard more than enough about this " Scotch dealer out of brimstone and fire."

Chief Justice. Mr. Cobbett, this is harsh language to use of a minister of the gospel.

Mr. Cobbett. I like, my Lord, to call things by their right names ; a cat, as the old adage goes, is but a cat all the world over.

Mr. Parsons. What, then, is the opinion, Mr. Cobbett, that you have formed of Mr. Irving and his preaching ?

Every body, Sir, must know that ; for every body reads Cobbett ; the very children must have got it by heart.

Well, but a good thing, you know, can't be repeated too often—once more if you please ?

Well, then—" The exhibition now going on at Hatton-garden every Sunday, is far more contemptible than any thing ever seen in the Catholic church. I have heard, indeed, of the women following the preaching and laughing Capuchins of Rome ! but I never heard of any thing else resembling this Hatton-garden show ; at which, it is said, Mr. Canning and other ministers attend. This preacher has been described to me as having a fine voice, being very eloquent, full of the spirit of grace, six feet two inches high, shoulders of breadth in proportion, long black hair, and a beard like a German scrubbing-brush. The church is advertised in the newspapers, almost in direct terms. Tickets are said to be sold for half-a-guinea. To hear this man bawling about ' *the level lake of fire,*' ' *the worm that dieth not,*' and ' *the flame that is not quenched ;*' to hear this stuff bawled out in a harsh Scotch accent, people run, and push, and squeeze, and strive, as if they were endeavouring to get from a house on fire. They run to his *fire* with as much eagerness as they would run from another fire. The *Morning Chronicle* frequently entertains us with stories about the credulity and gullibility of Roman catholics. That which I have just described is now actually going on in London. The audience consists partly of ministers of state, and of members and peers of parliament. This *great brimstone merchant* has the most fashionable part of the metropolis for his auditory. Here we have a specimen of the fruit of that light which the *Chronicle* tells us is in the Protestant mind. Can the *Chronicle* cite any instance in which Roman catholic folly has surpassed this ?"

But you are aware, Mr. Cobbett, how much the protestant mind has fallen from its former " *high estate.*" Have you not read how "*our soul is smitten with grief and shame,*" to remark how in this latter day, in this fag end of the thread of human existence, Revealed Wisdom hatn fallen, fallen, fallen, and along with her fallen the great and noble character of men?

All stuff—stuff—stuff, Sir: the common-place of quacks and impostors.— Mr. Irving tells you that nine-tenths of the people of England *know nothing at all* of the truths of Revelation. There is nothing new, however false, in this. There are *two hundred and eighty preachers* already roaming about the country preaching the same sort of nonsense. They speak of the English people as Heathen ; as " *destitute* persons," destitute of all knowledge of the Lord ! They call the places neglected villages, and they assert that these people : that is to say, a very large part of the people of England, are without the knowledge of God in this world. This Society has its head-quarters at the " Home Missionary Rooms, 18, Aldermanbury, London ;" and it has four Secretaries, whose names are Cobbin, Dunn, Moore, and Millar. The very existance of such a society, in a country paying tithes to the amount of six or seven millions a year, is a scandal without parallel. Here is a Church, collecting its tithes by the aid of soldiers ; and here is a society, putting into print and publishing that they have under their care, *two hundred and seventy-four villages*, containing a population of ninety-five thousand, three hundred and forty-four souls, *who enjoy no means of evangelical instruction.* " What then," say they, (and Mr. Irving but imitates their cant,) " must be the *general state of* *the villages in England."* The *Christian heart shudders* at the thought!—Sir, either this is true, or these are most impudent vagabonds. If it be true, what a pretty Church we have, after our two hundred years of *reformation!* If it be false, what a pretty state we are in with two hundred and eighty, (for that is the number that they say they have) of bawling **** * ** of this one description, going about England to *introduce the people to a knowledge of God!* Augustine, when he landed in Kent with his forty monks, had, I am sure, too much modesty to speak of the English of that day, as these impudent vagabonds speak of them now; and that in print too, and as bold as brass. They have no scruple to declare that the agricultural population of England is in a perfectly *heathenish* state.

But if they did not do this, Mr. Cobbett, what success would they have?

Oh! to be sure, money is collected by these heathen converters. *Money* is always included; for their object is to *live without work;* and to do this, they must have money. Accordingly, they plead most pressingly for money. They, in various publications, in pamphlets, in sheets, in half sheets, in quarter sheets, and in single leaves, set forth in grand array, the works of grace and salvation, that they are performing. But, then, they are in *want of money*. If they had but *money*, they would soon extirpate all the *heathenishness* of the poor souls who are now perishing. But without money what can they do!

Cross-examined by Mr. Phillips.

You know the Times newspaper, Mr. Cobbett?
The b——y old Times?—Oh yes—none better.
Do you ever write for it?

I have written all its best articles for a long time past; I wrote those famous articles about the queen, which raised its circulation from 3,000 to 20,000 in one week. To do it justice, however, I must say, that I don't think the stupid numsculls who manage it knew they were written by me: if they had, they would rather have been smothered to death (to make use of one of their own favourite similies), under the thousand and one quires they printed daily at that time, than have adopted them. But I have a way of my own, Sir, of managing these things. I can do other people's work for them, and make them say and do what I please, without their knowing or suspecting any thing of the matter.

Another *Brownie o' Brodsbeck,* I suppose.
Something of that, i' faith.
Well, Brownie, will you tell us one thing more? Was it not you who wrote that clever article in The Times, about Mr. Irving, beginning " there is a fashion in every thing—in wigs and bonnets," and so forth?
Yes—every word of it.
You swear that?
Broil me on a gridiron if it was not.

Editor of the Literary Chronicle, examined by
MR. PARSONS.

Do you know any thing, Sir, of the Rev. Defendant, what he is, and whence he came?

Mr. Irving, Sir, is a young man, a native of Annan in Scotland, who was for some time an assistant preacher to Dr. Chalmers of Glasgow, until both the Doctor and his colleague having *calls*, left their flocks to seek other shepherds. Dr. Chalmers was *called* to a professorship in a northern university. Mr. Irving was called, (and what Scotsman ever refused such a *call?*) from the bleak mountains of Scotland to the more fertile vineyards of the south, to that land flowing with milk and honey—the British metropolis.

Well, Sir, how has he fared since his arrival in this land of milk and honey?

" Some nine moons wasted," he was seated in the Caledonian chapel in Cross Street, Hatton Garden—a place of worship formerly known by the name of the *Gaelic* Chapel.

Gaelic! Does Mr. Irving preach in Gaelic?

Oh, no, Sir. It was found out by some *honest* folks, that the Gaelic language, however sonorous and mellifluous it may be in the long deep glens of the Highlands, is, in the polished streets of the metropolis, one of the most barbarous and intolerable jargons ever known to the tongue of man.* It was therefore resolved that there

---

* Absolutely what was stated at one of the meetings about Mr. Irving's call to the Caledonian chapel.—REPORTER.

should be no more preaching in Gaelic, but that a call should be given to Mr. Irving to come and proclaim the glad tidings of the gospel in Gallovidian English.

Or rather, I fancy, Sir, the resolution to call Mr. Irving was made first, and the reason for it came afterwards?

Not unlikely.

And what has become of the poor Gaelic folks in London who don't understand English? Have they been turned adrift without a pastor, and left to perish for lack of instruction?

Oh, Sir, nobody but porters and the like speak Gaelic only; and who cares for their perishing? Give me, says Mr. Irving, your "imaginative men, and political men, and legal men, and medical men." What indeed would the society of saints be worth, if it were made up only of Scotch caddies, Highland porters, Kentish gipseys, West Country bargemen, Welsh miners, and the like?

Mr. Irving preaches then only to people of high degree, such as your poets and statesmen, and lawyers and physicians?—Yes.

But how has he contrived to make these people run after him so?

Why the art is simple enough. Mr. Irving saw that in London preachers are followed not so much for their talents and attainments, as for their apparent zeal and the violence of their denunciations; that the more lustily a minister preaches damnation to his followers, the more eagerly he is followed, and every word he drops caught, as if

it were manna from heaven. He saw the higher
classes heedless of religion because their preachers
preached nothing but peace, peace: he saw the
lower cramming conventicles to the very ceiling,
because they heard of nothing there but fire, fire.
He reasoned, and reasoned correctly, that as the
poor crowded to chapels in proportion as their
sins were denounced, the rich would do the same,
and that he had only to attack the vices and follies
of the fashionable world to become popular : he
did so, and has succeeded.

Is this then the whole secret of his success ?

No ; another secret of his popularity is, that he
does not confine himself to attacking the higher
classes in the abstract: he singles out individual
characters—he thus takes advantage of that weak-
ness of human nature, the love of scandal, and
is the very " John Bull " of the clergy.

Has not curiosity also some share in the matter ?

Undoubtedly. His chapel is every Sunday a
gallery of beauty and fashion ; and while some of
the nobility and gentry are prompted by curiosity
to see and hear a preacher become popular by the
boldness of his denunciations, no inconsiderable
portion of his auditors are collected in the hopes
of seeing some Royal Duke or Princess, some
Minister of State, the famed Lady A. or the
beauteous Miss B.

But do you mean to say that Mr. Irving is a
man of no talents ?

Certainly not, he is a man of considerable talents, but they have been sadly overrated. He is

read well in books, but has not studied men ; his reasoning is superficial ; his judgment indiscreet ; his taste bad ; his conceit overwhelming ; his assurance most unblushing ; he is, in short, nothing but a sounding brass, a tinkling cymbol ; or, to call things by their right names, a mere scold.

You say he is well read in books. Do you mean that it should be inferred, that he shines in borrowed plumes ?

Not so exactly ; I have met with little in his volume of what we call plagiarism. Indeed, the only instance worth remarking is, after all, very excusable. " I wish," says Mr. Irving, " *that I had a dwelling place in every bosom.*" Sweet ecstatic idea ! but borrowed, as you will see, Sir, from the following passage of the Don Juan of that " woe-begone and self-tormented, wretched man," Lord Byron, as Mr. Irving calls him :—

> I love the sex and sometimes would reverse
> The tyrant's wish " that mankind only had
> One neck, which he with one fell stroke might pierce."
> My wish is quite as wide, and not so bad,
> And much more tender, on the whole, than fierce ;
> It being—(not now, but only while a lad)
> That womankind had but *one rosy mouth,*
> To kiss *them all* from north to south.

(much laughter : fans in requisition in the gallery.)

Cross-examined by MR. PHILLIPS.

You keep a common establishment, Sir, for giving characters ?

E

I edite a weekly Review, Sir.

Which every body knows is the same thing, Sir. Go down.

The Editor of the Album examined by Mr. Macvicar.

Were you at the Scottish Church in Hatton Garden, on Sunday, the 6th of July ?—I was.

What sort of audience did you find collected ?

I was surrounded on every side by faces well known upon town in every way.

For what purpose did they seem assembled ?

They were evidently brought there by some strong and peculiar motive ; but the general buzz and hum of different conversations, plainly proved that the motive was not to pray to God. There was none of that staid and decorous aspect and manner which, in those who cannot be called devout, supply an appearance fitted to the place. The company were evidently come to see a show, and they conversed with one another till the show began.

When was that ?

Just at eleven, a sort of motion and movement through the assemblage, told that Mr. Irving was entering. He had some difficulty in making his way to the pulpit, the stairs of which were covered with gaily dressed ladies. The service commenced by Mr. Irving reading a hymn, which was immediately afterwards sung by the clerk and the children of the Caledonian school.

How were you impressed at first with Mr. Irving's style of officiating?

I was disappointed. His voice seemed to have little modulation or tunefulness. I was still more displeased with the manner in which he read, it being with extreme pompousness of tone and contortion of countenance.

Did he improve as he went on?

Far from it. When he delivered the prayer, his eyes were forcibly closed; his mouth was drawn into an expression so pompous as almost to be farcical; the enunciation was studied and stilted to the last degree; the gesture was ungraceful throughout, and often vehement, and the matter was a succession of scriptural phrases linked together by language, aiming not very happily at the same style. Mr. Irving, I said to myself, means to make his prayer impressive by this manner: it is a pity he does not know that it is impossible to be impressive and unnatural at the same time. The prayer was concluded by the Lord's prayer, and the way in which he gave this was perfectly sufficient, I thought, to decide his taste and manner.

How was that?

It was mouthed, I might almost say, ranted, in the manner in which we are accustomed to hear the mock invocation in the *Critic*, spouted upon the stage—the face was more than usually contorted—the voice was more than usually violent and unequal—and the gesture! Oh! heavens! such gesture! During the preceding prayer, Mr. I. had stood chiefly with the arms slightly protruded from the body, and crossed by the right hand clasping the left arm about half way between the wrist and the elbow ; but this curious, and somewhat awkward posture, was changed when he commenced the Lord's Prayer, into one still more curious, and far more awkward. The arms were placed close by the sides, but raised perpendicularly from the elbow, with the hands erect.

Now, Sir, if you please, for the sermon—What did you think of that ?

I am no divine, Sir, and can say nothing of the matter of doctrine that it involved.

You can tell us, however, what you think of him as an orator, if not as a theologian ?

I had heard, Sir, a good deal of the peculiarity of diction, which Mr. Irving has adopted after the model of Jeremy Taylor, and the other old writers of our Church. It was, as it had been represented to me, and its effect was also what I had anticipated it would be. The diction which he employs is not now in use ; and it consequently appears affected, unnatural, and therefore unimpressive, He uses the third person singular of the verb, according to the old form,—for instance, he says, "it hath"—"it doth"—"it cometh"—"it goeth"— &c., and he employs a consonant obsoleteness of diction.

But of what sort was the substance of his sermon ?

The discourse, Sir, was one flood of inappropriate and bombastic language ;—extravagant without be-

ing in the least degree poetical ;—furious, without
even for a moment being forcible.   I could recog-
nize no deep thought—no fine images—nothing
pathetic—nothing impressive : his style was over-
charged with metaphor to the utmost degree ; but
his metaphors are nearly always false and broken.
During the whole sermon, which lasted an hour
and five-and-twenty minutes, there was scarcely
any image which was perfect, and positively, not
one, which remained impressed upon the mind by
its beauty, terseness, and truth.

How did he deliver the sermon ?

The manner of delivery, Sir, displeased me as
much as the composition.   The Lord's Prayer
had prepared me for a good deal, but I had no
conception that it was possible, any thing like the
violence of enunciation and gesture which Mr.
Irving displayed, *could* have been used in the pulpit ; or, indeed, anywhere else.   Mr. Irving's solemnity, is vehemence ; Mr. Irving's passion, is fury ;
and he is not guided in these bursts of convulsive
frenzy by the matter which he is delivering.   He
throws himself into all the variations of attitude,
which are consistent with every one of them being
ungraceful—his hands are clenched—the sweat
starts from his brow—his whole frame shakes—
and his voice comes forth with a quivering sound
from the extremity of his agitation ; and all this,
at a passage where manly earnestness was all that
was needed, or indeed, admissible.

Can you give us an example ?

When speaking of the Omnipotence of God,

that the whole universe was in His person, as he
pronounced the word *universe*, he absolutely
waved his arm round and round above his head,
in a manner, which is usual only when the hand
contains a hat, and the mouth is uttering huzza!
huzza! My friend Cruickshank, who was with
me, was constantly whispering into my ear, " What
a subject! capital! admirable !" His mischievous
pencil was at work the whole time, catching the
oddities and contortions of the preacher.

Perhaps you could shew the court some of these
sketches.

Here are some.—[Witness produced several of
these sketches done on the back of small address
cards. They were handed about the Court, and
kept it for several minutes in a general roar of
laughter. The editor of the Album has been kind
enough to permit us to have them engraved for
this report. The preacher is exhibited in five
different attitudes :—1st. The Glance Penetrating. 2d. The Knock it into Them. 3. The Solemn Invocation. 4. Solemn Invocation after
another manner. 5. The Crown All.]

Have you any thing farther, Sir, to add to your
evidence ?

I ought to observe that Mr. Irving's obliquity
of vision, of which so much is said, is worse than
that which is called a *squint*, and varies according
to the direction in which he looks. I came away,
upon the whole, lost in wonder, not at the noto-
riety which Mr. Irving has gained, for his style is
very much *ad captandum*, but at the report which

I had heard (but which I must say I now doubt), that some of our most really eloquent men have spoken of him in high praise.

The Printer of the Liberal examined by Mr. Parsons.

Have you, among the contributors to your " Verse and Prose from the South," any " well-wishers to religion and good order ? "

We have *one* queer fellow who calls himself so ; but I do not know what to make of him. He is, for all that, constantly in the company of ———— and ———— and ————.

Is he not in the practice of haunting churches and chapels a good deal ?

He has been hearing Mr. Irving several times of late ; and yet is constantly abusing him. The Caledonian Chapel, he says, resembles a booth at a fair ; and the pulpit, a stage, for a tall, raw-boned, hard-featured, impudent Scotch quack, to twang through the nose indecency, blasphemy, and sedition.

The things, probably, which take him there so often. Did he give you any instance of Mr. Irving's indecency ?—None.

Of his sedition ?—None.

Of his blasphemy ?

Yes, of something like it, at least. He mentioned that he had heard Mr. Irving, at one time, describe the God of natural religion as like the great desert—dry, disagreeable, comfortless, deadly—where no one wished to dwell ! No one, be insisted, could venture upon this gross insult to the God of nature (whom he apprehended to be also the God of Christians), without that strong obliquity of mental vision, that can keep natural religion in one eye and revealed religion in the other : look grave on the parent, and fulsome on the daughter. Mr. Irving had at another time, he said, asserted, by an impudent figure of speech, that the God of Mercy was like Alsatia, *where the scum of mankind took refuge ! !*

But all this does not prove Mr. Irving to be what he called him, " an impudent Scotch quack ? "

No ; but he mentioned another thing which does. He heard Mr. Irving issue a proclamation in the name of the King of Heaven, appointing himself crier of the court, beginning with a To wit, to wit ; and ending with damnation *to all those who do not go to hear him.*

The EDITOR OF THE BRITISH PRESS *examined.*

Are you " *A member of the established church ?*
Yes.
Have you inquired into the merits of Mr. Irving?
Yes, most particularly.
What is your opinion of him ?
I think him quite over-rated. Every page of his orations bears the stamp of a mind perfectly bewildered : we have a jargon of words with an utter barrenness of ideas ; there is no coming at his meaning, for he addresses himself neither to

the head nor to the heart, and contributes nothing either to enlighten the one, or improve the other. He delivers himself in a dialect so studiously quaint and affected, as to be for the most part wholly unintelligible. He rolls his sentences one over another, with an utter disregard to any thing like logical order or consecutive arrangement. If the reader passes them over rapidly, it is so far well; but if he pauses over any one of them, to discover its tendency or examine its truth, he will find that it is either so indefinite as to lead to nothing, or that when understood it leads to conclusions which no sound mind can admit. He delights not merely in rhetorical exaggeration of matters of fact; his discourses are full of idiotic trash, that any man of decent understanding would be ashamed of. He appears as if he sat down to write (to use a proverbial phrase of his country) with a *bee in his bonnet.* What man, for example, unless the faculties of his mind were disturbed, could run on in such a strain as the following :—
" *Masterful men,* or the *masterful current* of opinion, hath *ploughed* with the word of God, and the *fruit* has been to *inveigle the* mind into the exclusive admiration of some few *truths,* which being *planted* in the belief, and *sacrificed* to in all religious expositions and discourses, have become popular *idols,* which *frown heresy and excommunication* upon all who dare stand for the unadulterated, uncurtailed testimony. *Such Shiboleths every age hath been trained to mouth ;* and it is as much as one's religious character is worth, to think that

F

the doctrinal Shiboleths of the present day may not include the whole contents and capacity of the written word. But, truly, there are higher fears than the fear even of the religious world ; and greater loss than the loss of religious fame. Therefore, craving indulgence of you to hear us to an end, and asking the credit of good intention upon what you have already heard, we summon *your whole unconstrained man* to the engagement of reading the word ; — not to authenticate a meagre outline of opinions elsewhere derived, but to prove and purify all the sentiments *which bind the confederations of life ;* to prove and purify all the feelings which instigate the actions of life ; *many* to annihilate ; many to implant ; *all* to regulate and reform :—*to bridle the tongue till its words come forth* in unison with the word of God, and to *people* the whole soul *with the population* of new thoughts, which that word reveals of God and man—of the present and the future."

Voilà un chef-d'œuvre digne de notre siecle !

And this is the orator of Hatton Garden, who can only be heard with admission tickets ?

Yes ; Mr. Irving professes to address himself to a blind and senseless generation, but he seems to have caught the distemper he came to cure.

Fools that we are, like Israel's sons of yore,
The calf ourselves have fashion'd, we adore ;
But let true Reason once resume her reign,
This idol will become a calf again.

Editor of the Pulpit, examined by MR. MACVICAR.

I understand, Sir, you have lately established a censorship over the pulpits of the metropolis ?
Yes.
Your attention must, of course, have been particularly drawn to the exhibitions of Mr. Irving, in Hatton Garden ?—It has.
Tell us, pray, how Mr. Irving ranks as a preacher?
Mr. Irving himself, Sir, claims to be like no other living preacher on this side of the Tweed ; at least he has come to set *" an example"* to the whole body of the English clergy, of all denominations ; for so exceedingly deficient have they all been in the performance of their sacred functions, that according to him, there are *nine-tenths* of every class who know *nothing at all* about the truths of revelation.   Our popular leaders, he tells us, " finding no necessity for strenuous endeavours and high science in the ways of God, but having a gathering host to follow them, deviate from the ways of deep and penetrating thought— refuse the contest with the literary and accomplished enemies of the faith—bring a contempt upon the cause in which mighty men did formerly gird themselves to the combat—and so cast the stumbling-block of a mistaken paltryness between enlightened men and the cross of Christ !
Do you deem the pulpit a place for such reflections as these ?

By no means, Sir; I take it to be a gross prostitution of the privilege which the pulpit gives to preachers of saying what they please, and having *all the saying to themselves*, to reflect in this manner on one's fellow labourers in the ministry. Mr. Irving is besides but a young labourer, and as yet almost a stranger in this country; and it ill becomes one of such few years and limited experience thus to stalk forth, dispensing his censures on all around him, and holding himself up as the only model for universal imitation.

But may not the clergy, Sir, stand really in need of some such example being held up to them?

No, Sir; it is sheer ignorance which makes Mr. Irving vaunt so. Were he at all acquainted with the state of religion in the community where his lot is now cast, with what has been done, and is doing in it, to promote the cause of Christ; had he heard one out of ten of all the clergymen whom he calumniates in the mass *without hearing them,* he would never have spoken so falsely as he has done.

It would seem then, that Mr. Irving has erred merely from want of information?

Not so entirely. Mr. Irving is ignorant, not so much for want of opportunities of knowing better, but from a vanity and self-sufficiency which have prevented him from availing himself of those opportunities he has had. He thinks he has nothing to learn, and that nobody knows more; he goes on expatiating, when his first step should be to inquire. The attitude which he assumes is that

of the Pharisee, " Stand by thyself—touch me not
—I am more holy than thou."

You can tell us, perhaps, what the Scriptures
say of this sort of professors?

When our Redeemer commanded one of his
disciples to follow him, the latter asked what his
fellow disciple should do?   Most just and striking
was the reproof contained in our Lord's answer—
" If I will that *he* tarry till I come, *what is that to
thee?*   FOLLOW THOU ME."   So I would say to
Mr. Irving :—Even admitting all you say to be
true of your fellow disciples, " *what is that to
thee?*"   What is it to the great truths you have
undertaken to enforce, that others do not enforce
them after your fashion, or to your taste?   Do *you*
expound them as you think they ought to be expounded ; do *you* take care to do justice to the
" gathering host" that follows you ; be contented
to lay up for yourself a crown of glory that fadeth
not ; and snatch not with a rude and invidious
hand the wreath from the brow of your fellow disciple.   " If I will that he tarry till I come, *what
is that to thee?   FOLLOW THOU ME."

But has not Mr. Irving actually " *set the example
of two new methods* of handling religious truth?"
I allude to his Orations and Argument.

The *titles* are new, Sir, and that is all.   The orations and arguments themselves are like any other
discourses from the pulpit, except only that they
are not so formally divided and subdivided as sermons commonly, though by no means invariably,
are.   All that Mr. Irving says about the one me-

thod being " after the manner of the ancient oration," and the other " after the manner of the ancient apologies," I look upon to be exceedingly after the manner of the Fudge Family. Mr. Irving has a *modest* aversion to be thought in the least like any body else of his order ; he won't be called a writer of *sermons*, because all other clergymen are writers of sermons ; and this, Sir, is the real secret of the matter.

You have said, that were Mr. Irving acquainted with the state of society in this country, he would not talk so falsely as he has done. Do you mean then to deny that the oracles of divine wisdom " have fallen into a household commonness, and her visits into a cheap familiarity," that there is an " abeyance of intellect, a dwarfish reduction of the natural powers of men ; that, in short, nearly all the Christian world have " drifted away from that noble, manly, and independent course which, under steerage of the word of God, they might have safely pursued ?"

All a rhapsody of abuse, Sir. I would merely oppose to it *the truth*—the known and undeniable truth. I assert with perfect confidence (and I am no offended gownsman, but an unpretending layman, who would wish the very worst to have their due) that in no period in the history of this country, was revealed wisdom studied and expounded in a purer spirit, and with a happier effect on the lives of men, than it is at the present moment. With Mr. Irving there is nothing

like the " olden time ;" but I know of no olden
time when the great body of the people ranked
higher in the scale of morals and intelligence than
they do now.   I have read of times when they ate
more bacon and pudding, and drank more ale, and
were better clothed than they have lately been ;
but at no time that I ever read or heard of, was
the bulk of our community more orderly and
well-behaved, more morally and religiously inclined, more given to rational pursuits, more beings of mind, than they are now.

But Mr. Irving gives you facts.   He tells you
" their holidays are days of dissipation, their cups
crowned with licentious and blasphemous talk,
their raptures intoxication and brutal excess,
our fairs scenes of iniquity scandalous to be
looked upon, our intemperance proverbial over
the world, our prize fights a cruel game elsewhere never played at, our forgeries, our thefts,
our murders, not surpassed if equalled in the
most barbarous lands."   " The innocent sports of
our villages for which weary labour was want to
relax himself, the cheer and contentment which
blessed the interior of our cottages, and the
plenty and beauty which beamed around their
walls, the home bred comfort and cleanliness,
with all the Arcadian features of old English
life, live," he assures us, " no longer, save in the
tales of ancestry ;" and much he bewaileth, that
" hard and well earnt labour, broken with fierce
gleams of jollity and debauch, poor house dependence and poor-house discontent, nocturnal

adventures of the poacher, and the smuggler, and the depredator ; Sabbath breakings, Sabbath sports, and Sabbath dissipations, are now become the characteristics of our city and our rustic people."

But specks, at best, Sir, on the face of society. It is absurd and fallacious to convert them into a general picture. Mr. Irving talks of *facts* Sir ! I too would appeal to facts, and to some of the most recent which have come under public observation, with respect to the character and conduct of the lower orders. Will Mr. Irving shew us in all his " olden time," any example of such temperate behaviour on the part of thousands of men in the humblest walks of life, assembled to oppose a measure which they conceived was about to deprive them and their wives and children of bread, as has just been exhibited by the weavers of Spitalfields? Or will he show us, in all his " olden time," the whole workmen of a town turning out for a rise of wages, as is now the case at Knaresborough, assembling daily in immense multitudes, yet committing no violence nor outrage, and closing their meetings at night-fall, with the singing of psalms to that God who delivereth the poor and needy, and riddeth them out of the hand of the wicked.

Does not Mr. Irving elsewhere in his " argument," admit the constantly increasing improvement which the Christian spirit is producing in society?

Yes, explicitly enough. For example :—" In

this land, saith he, Christians " have disarmed
the thigh of its weapon, and procured revenge to
be taken out of the hands of the injured into the
hands of the upright judge ;—they have made
reformation to be acknowledged as the only object of punishment; they have abolished the
divine right of kings to have their will out of sub-
jects ;—they have almost got adultery to be acknowledged as the only righteous cause of di-
vorce ;—they have made the accommodation of
others to be sanctioned as the basis of polite-
ness ;—the spirit of government they have forced,
by sundry desperate efforts, to become equitable,
open, and disclosed, instead of being, as in the
Italian and other continental states, crooked and
intriguing. From all which it is manifest, that in
the force of heaven-directed will, there is a
staunchness, an intrepidity, and a long-suffering,
which brings out equity triumphant against injustice, and liberty against wilfulness, forming a
wall of shields around whatever is good in human
laws,—*smiting, as with a constant battering ram,
against every thing which is evil.*"

How is it that Mr. Irving is betrayed into such
gross contradictions and inconsistencies?

It all arises, Sir, from his egregious vanity. The
truth seems to have escaped from him in spite of
himself; for recollecting very shortly after, that
were it to pass as an admitted fact, that the doc-
trines of Christianity, as they have been hitherto
preached in this country, have been " *smiting
us with a constant battering ram, against every*

thing that is evil," there must of course be less
call than he imagines for the aid of the minister
of the Caledonian church, and his new methods ;—
anxious to guard against any such dangerous admission in the way of business, he falls again into
the lamenting strain. " Oh," says he, " that the
spirit of the ancients would rise again and shame
these modern men who go dreaming, &c." All
this affected lamentation, Sir, is made for no
other purpose than to furnish one opportunity
more of telling the world what a different sort of
example Mr. Irving means to exhibit. " Moved
by their lethargy and indifference, I do challenge
them, &c." I shall " try another method," I " shall
strike a note to thrill the drowsy chambers of the
soul, and awaken it from its fatal slumbers."
Alas, proud boaster ! he thinks he has got the
world on his shoulders ! The men he talks of
shaming, the men he charges with lethargy and
indifference, are the men of the battering ram,
who as he hath himself before confessed, have
in their might brought out " equity triumphant
against injustice, and liberty against wilfulness,
forming a wall of shields around whatever is good
in human laws."

Mr. Irving's censures are not, I believe, confined to the clergy. Does he not blame alike our
poets, our men of science, our politicians ?

Yes, his shafts fly thick. In poetry he tells us
there is none who " inditeth a song unto his
God." In philosophy, the palace of the soul, men
see in the rough and flinty faces of the cloud-

capt rocks, more delectable images to adore, than in the revealed countenance of God;" and in politics, there are men to whom the Liberal, or John Bull, (afar from me be such indecorous associations) " are more moving than the secrets of the Eternal." All these assertions, Sir, are the offspring either of downright ignorance, or of wilful misrepresentation. Mr. Irving talks as if he knew nothing of the people he was arraigning. We have, thank God, many pious poets, many pious philosophers, many pious politicians. There is nobody who sees and feels as Mr. Irving describes. His mode here as elsewhere, is to blow the bubble first, and then, at the slightest puncture of his lance, it falls to nothing.

After all, Sir, is there any thing strange or new in this chapter of lamentations?

Nothing, I confess. It savours all of the rankest common place—such common place as a man of Mr. Irving's pretensions to originality should have disdained. The goodness of the good old times, is the common cant of your self-righteous people, your ranters, and your jumpers. There is a lady of the name of Priscilla Hunt, who journeys about talking the same sort of extravagance. The chief difference between her and Mr. Irving, in this respect, is, that she does not ascribe the "*fallen*" state of men to precisely the same cause. In a report of one of this pious damsel's recent exhibitions which I have lately seen, her first complaint is, " of the lamentable state into which things had fallen, in consequence of

*the hissing of the serpent, the whispering of the
back-biter, and the lashing of the lying tongue.*"
I would say with this same Priscilla:—" But it
is of verity, my friends, that if people were
truly concerned for the well-being of the human
family and the good of their own souls ; all these
customs (namely of hissing and whispering, and
backbiting and lashing with the lying tongue,)
would necessarily vanish, and instead thereof
*boundless love would prevail, universal harmony
would predominate.*"

Your chief objection, Sir, to Mr. Irving, seems
to be to his vain boasting.   Have you told us the
worst you know of it ?—I fear not, Sir.

The egotism of Mr. Irving is unhappily not limited to a supreme disdain of other men's powers
and attainments ; it dares even to ascend beyond
this mortal sphere. He thinks so much of himself
as to be to all appearance habitually divested of
every thing like true Christian humility.   When
he speaks of the Almighty, the familiarity and
levity of the language he employs is at times
shudderingly revolting.   In one place we are
told that "God might be a *pattern* to all lawgivers;"
in another, that the laws of God, of Him who
is the source of all things, differ from all others
in *the originality* of their principles ; further on,
that God is all perfect " like the Apollo Belvi-
dere!!!" (a thrill of horror through the court). In
short, such is Mr. Irving's high opinion of his
Maker, that he does " not doubt of the AL-
MIGHTY's *force of character* to carry any thing

into effect." Then we have every now and then such expressions as " Oh, Heavens !" " Oh, my God !" " In the holy name of Christ, and the three times holy name of God !" " God send repentance, or else *blast* the powers they have abused so terribly."

You do not mean, surely, to impute to Mr. Irving intentional impiety in the use of these expressions ?

Certainly not. Few men have described more forcibly than Mr. Irving has done elsewhere, the majesty of heaven, and the immeasurable distance between man and his Creator; but it is to be gathered from the fact of his frequent forgetfulness of the reverence which is due to the Most High, that his descriptions have not been the result of a sufficiently heartfelt or abiding sense of man's insignificance, but have been produced very much like any other task or exercise which might be proposed to the imagination. Were Mr. Irving called upon to describe the Paradise of Mahomet, he would do it, I dare say, in language nearly as vivid as any in this book concerning the mansions of God. To exemplify to you that play of the imagination to which I allude, I may refer you to Mr. Irving's offer to create a new hell for men. You shudder, I perceive, at the impiety of the proposition, nor do I wonder at it. No man, who felt a becoming awe for the Omnipotent Creator, could even in imagination, thus dare to place himself on a level with God, in the creation of destinies for mankind. The words of the proposal Sir, are these :—

" Bring me all the classes of men upon the earth, and LET ME have the sorting and the placing of them upon this earth, and I *shall make hells for each one of them without further ado.* I would send the poets to bear burthens, and the porters to indite tuneful songs. The musicians I would appoint over the kennels, and the roving libertines I would station over the watch and ward of streets. I would banish the sentimentalists to the fens, and send the labourers of the fens to seek their food among the mountains ; each wily politician I would transplant into a colony of honest men, and your stupid clown I would set at the helm of state. But lest it may be thought I sport with a subject which I strive to make plain, I shall stop short, and give no farther proof of this *wicked ingenuity ; for sure I am, I could set society into such a hot warfare and confusion, as should, in one day, make half the world slay themselves, or slay each other, and the other half run up and down in wild distraction."*

And this is what Mr. Irving calls preaching the Gospel ?—Yes.

The opinion you entertain of him on the whole, is not, I presume, very favourable ?

It is not. No man who hears him, or who reads his works, can remain without a conviction that he is a man of more than ordinary talents ; but for my own part, I am not disposed to rate those talents half so highly as the author does himself. The self-sufficiency which Mr. Irving displays, is, of itself, an evidence of a mind not wonderfully elevated above the common level. He overrates himself as much from narrowness of intellect as from ignorance. He is not at all deeply read either in men or books; yet, for a person of his years, and with the opportunities he has had, he ought to know more than he does. His novelties are, for the most part, common places; his projects, revivals of things which have never ceased. He has imagination, but little judgment—Jacob's dream, without the ladder. He is all sail, without ballast. His views want depth, steadiness, uniformity, consistency. He is an imaginer of premises, and jumper to conclusions. He is one of those who flatter themselves that they have such an intuitive knowledge of things, that they may spare themselves all the vulgar fatigue of inquiry? a single glance serves their purpose, and it is on single facts accordingly that all their reasoning turns. He would be a meteor in literature; for there is nothing, he tells you, like books, but places his chief dependence for attracting the gaze of the multitude, not on writing better in the style of the age in which he lives, but on strutting in the antiquated robes of his great grandfather. We have read of a Bishop in the olden time, who played at shuttlecock in the pulpit in order to fix all eyes upon him : Mr. Irving would do the same if there were no other way of bringing a " gathering host" around him.

Do you think that it is for Christ's sake alone that he affects so much ?

I am afraid not. His censoriousness, his ostentation, his boastings, his denunciations, breathe all of something very different from the pure

Christian spirit. It is not strong writing occasionally in favour of the tenets of the Gospel, that will mark the sincere believer; the greatest infidel that lives may do the same. The faith of a man must be evidenced by all his habitual modes of expression, and habitual modes of acting; and more especially by meekness, by charity, by loving-kindness, before I, for one, can believe for one moment, that its home is seated in the heart.

Cross-examined by Mr. Phillips.

You have imputed to Mr. Irving *narrowness of intellect?* You have said that he is *not at all deeply read either in men and books ;* and that his views *want depth, steadiness, uniformity, consistency.* Now, Sir, will you have the goodness to look at this—[handing to the witness No. I. of the publication called the Pulpit]—and read to the Jury the passage which I have marked there on page 5.

Witness (reading) — " Mr. Irving is an *expounder of the first order*—(expressions of surprise throughout the Court) — whose knowledge of human nature, and imaginative insight into the ways of Providence, are such as enable him, with singular success, to vindicate the reasonableness and justice of these opposite destinies which the book of God unfolds to his erring creatures."

Mr. P. Well, Sir, out of thine own mouth I have refuted thee.

Witness. Allow me, Sir, to explain. When we

ventured on the opinion I have last read, we had only occasionally heard Mr. Irving *preach*; we had not read his sermons, for they were not then published: we had heard him too in one of his wiser and happier moods. He was expounding the principles on which the distinction is to be drawn between the righteous and the wicked, as laid down in Matt. ch. xxv. v. 31. It was a vigourous, straight-forward, and uncompromising exposition of the divine law on the subject, and distinguished by comparatively but few ebullitions of conceit or spleen. It won him that esteem and admiration which we expressed so warmly at the time, and which it has given us pain to be obliged to retract. We little anticipated that it would make its appearance in print, in such exceptionable company as it does. We did not expect to see the sincere Christian pastor affiliating with the braggarts and mountebanks of this selfish world; affecting exclusive gifts and inspirations; seeking to build a name to himself, by casting down every high and venerated name around him. We fondly hoped that he would have adhered to the straight line of pastoral duty, and made it his great and single ambition to gather the flock entrusted to his care, unto the bosom of their Redeemer. He has not done so: and therefore alone have we condemned him.

Editor of the New Evangelical Magazine examined by MR. PARSONS.

Have you heard Mr. Irving preach? Yes.

Will you favour the Court with your opinion of his style of oratory?

It is one of the most finished specimens of burlesque on the art of oratory that ever fell under my notice. When Demosthenes was asked what was the first point in oratory—

Oh! we know all about that. Have you reviewed his book?——No.

Do you mean to review it?——No.

Why not?

Because I could say nothing good of it.

Editor of the John Bull examined by Mr. SERJEANT BISHOP.

[The call for this witness produced a general buzz and movement throughout the assembly. Every one was on tiptoe to get a sight of him. " How provoking!" whispered Lady ——, so loud as to be heard by all the Court. " Here we have him now —but that confounded mask—there is still no telling who he is. I declare if I were down there I could tear it from his face." " He does not look old, Sir." " Nor so very young, Ma'am." " Nor so very frightful, my dear." "He is not tall," "not little," " not fat," "not lean," "no giant," "no pigmy," "no Hercules," " no Jack-a-dandy." What he was *not* every body could tell; what he *is* Miss Letitia B—— alone ventured to surmise. " As I shall declare," simpered the amiable creature, " he is—— just the height of dear Mr. D——."]

I understand, Sir, that your *forte* as a journalist consists in the successful exposure of what is vulgarly called *humbug*. Have you met with anything of that description lately in the neighbourhood of Hatton Garden?

Yes, Sir, with one of the most flagrant and disgusting pieces of humbug ever foisted upon the people of this metropolis.

To what do you allude, Sir ?

To the absurd fashion which has obtained of following a Scotch Presbyterian parson of the name of Irving. I was inclined to laugh at the folly at first as one which could not last, and which during a temporary prevalence would not be seriously mischievous, but soon felt called upon to look at the affair in a very different point of view.

You took it up then seriously ?

Yes. Bull pointed out how degrading, how theatrical, how laughable, how contemptible a thing it was to see such bustling and crowding, such scrambling, pushing and squeezing for admission—all to hear a great brawny Scotchman, with an accent as vulgar and abominable as Hume's, talk the most detestable nonsense that ever came from human lips. Bull shewed up the quack—described his Jewish appearance and black matted hair, and ludicrous obliquity of vision. Bull dissected the sort of stuff which men, orators, wits, senators, and statesmen, were said to countenance by their presence ; which crowds, following the example of those to whom the nation looks up, leaving their pews untenanted, and their own churches all but locked, were huddling helter-skelter, pell-mell to Hatton Garden, to hear, and to come away *delighted with,* as they were said to be.

What effect had your exposure?

It opened the eyes of the public to the Presbyterian quackery with which, at first, they were so surprisingly taken. The most zealous of Mr. Irving's adherents and followers began to repent of the rashness with which they had committed themselves by an avowal of their admiration. My Lord Erskine, indeed, went after this to hear him; but you may imagine what he took by his motion, when I tell you the words of the text—"He speaketh to the Jews words of comfort, but to *the Greeks,* foolishness." (A laugh, in which his Lordship joined.)

Was any attempt made to bolster up the defendant when thus assailed by your satire?

Yes. When he began to fall off from that tipsy popularity which for a week or two he had acquired, it became necessary for his brother quacks to lend their aid to keep up the humbug, by which, defection from the Established Church was to be promoted, and rant and cant exalted above reason and religion. The Rev. John Clayton, junior, of the Poultry Chapel, it appeared, had said that which follows, from the pulpit :—

" There has recently appeared in our metropolis, an extraordinary man, of whom I have endeavoured to suspend my opinion till I had seen and compared his promised production. And now, to what shall I compare him? I will liken him to a fine young eagle from the bleak regions of the north, which has lately escaped from the nest. His eye is piercing, and he can look at the solar orb : his pinions are strong, and capable of a lofty flight. At present he chiefly dwells among rocks and caverns, amidst wild and romantic scenes. Though he floats with some irregularity of movement over the ocean and plain above which he soars—though he pounces with indiscriminate eagerness upon his prey; and though, when he alights, he may sometimes strike his broad wings against the projecting points of the craggy cliffs— yet give him the fair opportunity to plume his feathers and renew his flight, and (if God still sustain him,) the evident tendency of his course is to direct the eyes and minds of the spectators to the 'sun of Righteousness,' and to those glorious skies in which that everlasting luminary shines.

"For my own part, I have been grieved to see a number of lesser birds, of meaner nest, of feebler wing, and harsher note, flocking around him, and attempting to impede his ascent by their flutterings, screams, and cries. I hope that you, my beloved people, will prove yourselves to be of a better brood. Refuse not to honour the man God has been pleased to honour. Pray that the church and the world may receive the benefit of his ministrations, and God have all the glory. At least, shake off from the wings of your spirits, the earthly dust of envy, malice, and all uncharitableness.

> " Pale envy, withering at another's joy,
> Which hates the excellence it cannot reach!"

Did you make any reply to this fine effusion ?

Yes; Bull proved that it was all noise and nonsense.—Ex. gr. "At present," says Mr. John Clayton, junior, "he dwells chiefly among rocks and caverns, amidst wild and romantic scenes." How could Mr. John Clayton tell such an abominable bouncer? The orator, as we all know, dwells chiefly in Cross-street, Hatton-garden, among houses and chimneys, between Saffron-hill and High Holborn. The nonsense these mountebank ranters prate is below any serious criticism.

Did your tilt at the Caledonian orator end there ?

No; Bull indited a ballad, to the tune of Nancy Dawson, which finished him.

You can perhaps favour the Court by singing the ballad?

Mr. Phillips objected to such an exhibition, as contrary to the decorum of the Court.

Mr. Serjeant Bishop knew of no difference, in common sense, between saying and singing. Certain he was, that he had heard many a speech *which was all sing-song*, and no objection made to it; some too which, though full of sound and pretension, were not worth the tenth part of *an old song*.

Mr. Parsons remembered a case in the Court of King's Bench, Ireland, where a defendant, accused of singing a seditious song, was permitted to sing it over again in Court, in order to convince the Jury that the meaning of it had been misapprehended.

The Chief Justice overruled the objection.

Bull then sung, with a very clear and melodious voice, the following ballad :—

DOCTOR SQUINTUM.

Come, Beaux and Belles, attend my song,
Come, join with me the motley throng,
The time is apt, the tide runs strong,
            Your hearts no longer harden.
The world at once is pious grown,
And vice a thing no longer known;
For *Doctor Squintum's* come to town
            To preach in Hatton Garden.

The Doctor is a charming man,
A good deal on the WHITFIELD plan,
Men's vices he doth plainly scan,
   Not delicately hint 'em.
A fire upon his flock he'll keep,
And treats them more like wolves than sheep,
Till some go mad—but more to sleep :
   Oh, charming Doctor Squintum !

Such crowds of fashion throng the door
With tickets numbered, to secure
" *Exclusion*" to the *Pious* POOR
   Who never pass the entry.
HUMILITY the Scot doth teach
In tones the hardest heart to reach :
But when he *condescends* to preach,
   'Tis only to the GENTRY.

The Chapel's like a playhouse quite,
When thronged on Mr. *Liston*'s night ;
The boxes, gall'ries, bursting tight,
   Besides a very full pit.
And there they crowd to hear their DOOM
From one who talks like DOCTOR HUME,
And works and jerks like LAWYER BROUGHAM,
   Exalted in a pulpit.

When wandering quacks expose their stuff—
Themselves not quite absurd enough—
They hire *Jack Pudding* fools to puff
   Their trash to ev'ry noodle.
So *Squintum*, zanies gets in pairs,
As other *Humbugs* do at fairs,
And *Montague* upon the stairs,
   Harangues with *Cock-a-Doodle!*

Small *Taylor* leaves his teeming board,
Saxe Cobourg quits his shining hoard,
And *Poodle Byng* gives up a Lord,
                    To join the pious jostle.
With lightening speed *Lord Sefton* flies,
And *Coke* contrives betimes to rise,
While little *Bennet* sits and cries,
                    At *Holborn's* high Apostle.

My Lord, the Duchess, and his Grace,
All join the scrambling melting race,
And Ministers in pow'r and place,
                    Whose names—we scorn to print 'em:
These leave their pastors in the lurch,
And much it grieves us in the search,
To find the *State* desert the *Church*
                    For such a thing as *Squintum.*

But vanity doth never know,
At what to stop, nor where to go,
His sermons are attractive, so
                    He undertakes to print 'em.
This last manœuvre spoils the whole,
For partisans, like *Mistress Cole,*
Peruse and cry—" God bless my soul !
                    " Are these by Doctor Squintum ?"

Like that Hibernian blazing star,
Great *Mr. Phillips* at the bar,
His metaphors his matter mar,
                    Nor does he care to stint 'em;
In holding forth he tops his school,
But *readers* find—(then being cool)
The sermon trash, the man a FOOL,
                    A very DOCTOR SQUINTUM.

Mr. Sergeant Bishop said, that he would here close his case. He had many other witnesses in attendance, of equal talent and respectability with those he had examined, who could bear similar testimony; but he conceived that he had already proved more than enough to entitle him to a verdict from the Jury on all the Counts of the Indictment.

THE DEFENCE.

Mr. Irving. "My Lords and Gentlemen of the Jury. While, in a humble dependance on Divine aid, I undertake my defence against the various charges now brought against me, much it dispiriteth me to think how this world's scorn constantly triumphs over every manly endeavour to speak to men of their eternal interests, in terms befitting the awful importance of the theme. No sooner doth a preacher or writer with any nerve appear, who might make invasion on Satan's reign, than that prince of darkness covers him with the disparagement of some hated name— calling him enthusiast, fanatic, or gospel quack, and so prevents his words from reaching to those places where the lust of the flesh, the lust of the eye, and the pride of life have their strongest holds,—or Satan raiseth up some strong-minded, light-witted scoffer to argue or laugh him down. Nay, of such he hath establishments—scholars, wits, and critics, who hate the very visage of a

I

genuine disciple of Christ, and are aye ready to
asperse any book which is marked with the sign of
the Cross, and send it into the arcana of oblivion.
And oh! the natural man loveth any thing better
than to hear of his new birth and regeneration,
and will take up with a pleasant song or idle tale
sooner than he will with the institutes of his own
salvation.　And, alas! there are multitudes who
cannot read what is written, and come not to
hear what may be spoken ; so that, Gentlemen, it
dispiriteth me while I address you, to think of
the difficulties which stand before my way, and
how abler men have endeavoured in vain, to beat
these difficulties down.

"Gentlemen of the Jury, it hath been my
wish to deal wisely between the reason of man
and the Revelation of God, steering wide of the
coarseness and cruelty with which dogmatical
theologians ride over the head of every natural
feeling and reasonable thought of doubting men.
To occupy this ground of mediating the matter
in dispute between the reasoning power of man
and the Revelation of Almighty God, I may have
given offence to both—to the one for not having
done its difficulties justice, to the other for having
too daringly intermeddled with the secrecy and
sacredness of its counsels.

"Gentlemen, I am but weak and feeble-minded
like other men ; begirt also with manifold engage-
ments, and invaded with the noise of this unrest-
ing place, and therefore I hope, from the sympathy of my fellow-mortals, forgiveness for any

injustice I may have shewn *them*. From the secret ear of God I shall seek for that forgiveness for which HE is to be feared, and that redemption for which HE is to be sought after.

"In casting my thoughts back on what I have said and written, I confess that I see many passages in which I have spoken with liberty of men who still live under their Maker's good providence and within the reach of his tender mercy. These I might easily have expunged, or now soften down or make atonement for ; but I would not, I cannot. For our zeal towards God and the common good, hath been stung almost unto madness by the writings of reproachable men, who give the tone to the sentimental and the political world. Their poems, their criticisms, their blasphemous pamphlets have been like gall and wormwood to my spirit, and I have longed to summon into the field some arm of strength which might evaporate their vile and filthy speculation into the limbo of vanity from whence it came.

"For which office, being satisfied that nothing less than omnipotent truth under leading of Almighty God will suffice, I am weary of the vain infliction of pains and penalties by the ruling powers, which doth but aggravate the evil by awakening sympathy in the bosom of all who dread that power should ever intermeddle with the free circulation of thought. Seeing that Truth which I revere, thus wounded both by friends and foes, I could not rest, but have spoken out my feelings wherever occasions offered, at the risk of offending the workers of evil, and those who by brute power endeavour to counterwork them.

" I have done so I say ; not, Gentlemen, that I am equal to the task, or have executed the task, but in the hope of summoning from the host of the Lord of Hosts some one (surely I cannot be mistaken that there are some such !) able and willing to take the field in the fair conflict of truth, and cast back into these blaspheming throats their vain bravadoes against the armies of the living God. One such spirit would do us more good than all the prosecutions and suppressions which all the law authorities of the realm can carry into effect.

" But, Gentlemen, I fear the worst; that the intrigues of policy and the weight of power will in this age totally expel from the two established churches all the virtue and vigour of mind from which such deeds can alone proceed.

" Sometimes again I hope the best ; that through the spirit of God working better understanding upon those powerful men who at present outwit religion with their policies, and strangle her with their power, the noble spirit which now lieth depressed in both, and especially in this establishment of England, will be extricated, and the Newtons and Scotts who still watch in her corners will yet have wide seas to administer, and provinces to watch over.

" But, alas ! this renovation long lingereth, and the enemy taketh advantage of its tardiness. If it linger however much longer, if our churchmen will not bestir themselves, I do hope that ere this realm, which is faint at both extremes, sick at the heart, and threatening to lay down its heavenly spirit of religion, some of those men who in our senates do both know and seek the Lord, will lift up their voice and make the calamity of England's and Scotland's wasted parishes and faded provinces to be heard in the ears of those whom God hath appointed to rule them in righteousness and holiness. Surely they mean not to await till we fall into the condition of prostrate Ireland. No ! that can never be ; for long ere then, the generous spirit of the south and the indignant spirit of the north will have eased them of those who trouble their prosperity.

" Oh ! it afflicts me to see this generation merging apace into a state of sensuality, the lowest to which human nature can be addicted. It hath its head-quarters in your splendid feasts and your park parades, in your Vauxhall, your operas, and your theatres. It is very hateful as it is exhibited in cities where it is stewed up in hot quarters, and revels away the hours of quiet night, and wastes upon feverish couches the hours of cheerful day. In the country it shews itself under fairer forms, wandering from stream to stream, climbing the brow of lofty mountains, seeking love in cottages, and doting over the face and charms of external nature. Ah ! in this shape it is a dangerous enchantment, for it taketh the forms of taste and poetry, and even affects the feeling of devotion ; but unless conjoined with

that spiritual life whereof I have discovered the
sources, it is vanity and vexation of spirit, and
hurries one through an exhausting variety to the
lethargy and tedium of overwrought excitement.
This, Gentlemen, is the form of sensual life, which
is prevailing at this day among our lettered and
reading people. It hath been promoted and
brought into maturity by the writings of Byron
and of Moore, who are high priests of the senses
and ministers of the Cyprian goddess, whose temples they have decorated with emblems of genius,
and disguised with forms of virtue, and surrounded with scenes of balmy freshness; but with all
its forms and decorations, it is the temple of im-
moral pleasure, and the source of its inward
shame is disgusting sensuality. It is very pitiful
to behold the hopes of a nation, the young men
and young women who are to bear up the ancient
honours of this godly and virtuous island, heark-
ening to the deceptions of such enchanters who,
being themselves beguiled, would fain bewitch
the intellectual, and moral, and spiritual being
of others.

"Am I to blame that I have endeavoured to
reach those sensualists with the tidings of spiritual
and everlasting life? Am I to blame that I have
directed their thoughts beyond the grave? Am
I to blame for carrying them beyond the yawning
gulf of dark immateriality, where they have vainly
sought to bury all fear and apprehensions of
the future; for exhibiting to them matter again
invested with spirit, eyeing the spiry flames and

the dun smoke of hell ; bathing on the liquid ele-
ment of fire, snuffing up the fumes of her sulphu-
reous bed, and at her heart a worm gnawing that
dieth not ?

" Much too doth it afflict me to behold some
men, who, in contrast to the true animal I have
just represented, claim for themselves the character of *intellectual* and *rational* men. I speak
not, Gentlemen, against intellect—I cannot find
in my heart to speak against it ; and, thanks be
to God, I am not called by my Christian calling
to do so. It is a handmaiden of religion, and
religion loveth to be adorned at its hands. The
intellectual or rational life is an exalted kind of
existence, to which true men in all ages have be-
taken themselves. They stand like towers of
strength athwart the desolation of ages that hath
swept over the reputation of the rest ; their names
are like the ruins of ancient temples and palaces
in a desert city, where a level bed of sand hath
hidden in darkness all meaner places. A Homer,
a Socrates, a Plato, an Archimedes, a Newton—
these are the giants of the soul, the plenipoten-
tiaries of intellect, who redeem the reputation of
the human race. These men cared not for their
body ; but, like St. Paul, they groaned under it,
and made their moan in the ear of God, who
listening to their prayer, gave them victory.
The intellect which is weighed down with a fleshly
load achieved its redemption ; it wandered abroad
into the regions of the handy works of God ; it
dived into the mysteries of the soul, and dis-

coursed over the fields of wisdom, inditing match-
less sayings, and dressing feasts of fancy and of
reason for all ages of mankind. They are the
royal priesthood of mind, sphered above the sphere
of Kings, great and glorious beyond all heroes,
and conquerors of the earth. After their example,
the true men amongst mankind have strove, setting
them up for the Apostles of their high calling;
and in this island we have had, in all ages, a succession of such men, who have collected libraries
which are the armouries of intellect, and founded
colleges which are its nurseries, and created honours which are its laurels.

" But must I speak the truth? Intellect is now
often a handmaiden of other mistresses, with whom
religion hath no fellowship;—of vanity, of carnal
pleasure, and of filthy lucre.—Go to the seats of
learning, which intellect decked for herself with
chaste and simple ornaments, where she dwells in
retirement from noise and folly, wooing medita-
tion under the cool shade, or forcing her to yield
her hidden secrets to midnight research and mor-
tification,—what find you generally but pomp
parading it under vain apparel; sense rejoicing it
over feast and frolic; youth doting upon outward
distinctions; and age doting on idle and luxurious
ease. Such are a sort of sacrilegious ministers in
the temple of intellect. They profane its shew-
bread to pamper the palate; its everlasting lamp,
they use to light unholy fires within their breast,
and to shew them the way to the sensual chambers of sense and worldliness.

" Am I to blame, Gentlemen, that against this sort of intellectual life I have proclaimed war? That I have shewn unto them that such abuse of God's gift, cannot abide his judgment? Nay, that for men so gifted, to set God at nought, and so to lust after worldly vanities, is to deserve to be twice condemned?

" Let religious people blame me, or not, I will declare, for I speak my thoughts freely and fearlessly, that if intellect, foregoing such worldly prizes, will for itself cultivate itself, and guard against self-idolatry, it will come by a *natural course* to speculate upon the invisible God, like Plato and Socrates, in the days of old, and the Bible will come to its hungering and thirsting after divine knowledge like a stream of water to the thirsty hart in a parched land ; and it will rear its house by the clear margent of the waters of life, and therein dwell till God do separate it into his nearer neighbourhood and closer fellowship. Such intellectual examinations, brought Locke and Newton, after they had exhausted the faculties of the mind in research, to lay them down at length and drink refreshment from the river of the Lord's revelations, and there to devote the whole enjoyment of their souls.

" But such intellectual creatures as find their beloved field a mere physical research, contented with any new thing in nature or in art, that is, your mere naturalists, often the weakest and idlest of men ; such others as are satisfied with the speculations of politics, and have their feast in the triumphs of a party, or in being themselves the leaders of a party; or such others, who gape with open mouth for whatever the daily press may serve them withal, devouring with equal relish, novels, poems, news, and criticism, and so they can hold discourse about such wrecks, which ever float upon the edge of oblivion's gulf, think they have purchased to themselves a good degree in intellect. Oh! what shall I say to such men? Why should it have fallen to my lot to rebuke such a generation? What right has such a reading and talking generation of beings to claim any place or degree in the world of intellect? Not that I undervalue such an employment as perusing what the mind of man is continually producing, but that I would estimate the value and duration of that sentimental life, in which so many pride themselves, and estimate it as a mere game or pastime of the faculties, a dissipation of the eye of the mind; a sort of life, which must pass away at death, for its food will then be at an end, and its excitement at an end; and in the spiritual and eternal world, with which it held no communion, it can expect to find no enjoyment, unless God, as hath been said,* for the sake of those that never could have mercy, or obeyed any word, should make himself ‘ an egregious liar.’

"Then, Gentlemen, there are your *moral men,* whose excellence consists in living after the rules

---

* Argument for Judgment to Come, p. 448.

and measures of truth, sacrificing the heart in obedience to the understanding, conforming the will to the deliberations of reason—am I to blame, that I have declared of these, that they are not excusable for refusing to enter into communion with God, and enrolling themselves under the banner of Christ, who is the great teacher of pure morals, the great martyr in their behalf, and their great rewarder? For though to them I have spoken in soft and gracious language, yet to them, no less than the others, the truth must be spoken, that this life of theirs, hath its limitation in the grave.

" Alas! alas! The common heart of man hath forsaken the revealed supremacy of God, and refused to be charmed withal. I testify, that there ascendeth not from earth a hosannah of her children, to bear witness in the ear of the upper regions to the wonderful manifestations of her God! From a few scattered hamlets in a small portion of her wide territory, a small voice ascendeth like the voice of one crying in the wilderness. But to the service of our General Preserver there is no concourse from Dan to Beersheba of our people; the greater part of whom, after two thousand years of apostolic commission, know not the testimonies of our God, and the multitude of those who do reject or despise them.

" Return we now to inquire whence this lamentable state of things arises. There is an *establishment* of physicians to make known the remedy unto the people, and there are houses open where the remedy is made known. But, alas! the people know not of the soul-consuming malady, and having none to tell them, they come not to be cured, while in their darkness Satan revelleth,— wasting them with lust, and pride, and quarrels. The men of God hardly speak above their breath, who were wont to ring doom and woe into every impeding minister of evil. They creep about under the colossal limbs of power, and cry mercy, instead of denouncing vengeance. It is an age in which the ancient spirit is well nigh extinct. It is not that the powers of man are weakened, for I thus far agree with one of the witnesses you have heard this day, that there never was an age more patient of research, or more restless after improvement. Neither is it that the Spirit of God hath become backward to his help, or the Word divested of its truth. The great reason of the decadence I lament, is our treating the Word not as the all-accomplished wisdom of God. Faith should brood with expanded wings over the whole heavenly legend, imbibing its entire spirit. What hath it become? A name to conjure up theories and hypotheses upon. Duty likewise hath fallen into a few formalities of abstaining from amusements and keeping up severities, instead of denoting a soul girt with all its powers for its Maker's will. Religion, also a set of opinions and party distinctions separated from high endowments, and herding with cheap popular accomplishments, a mere serving maid of every-day life, instead of being the mistress of all earthly, and the preceptress of all heavenly sentiments, and the very queen of all high gifts, and graces, and perfections, and every walk of life !

" Gentlemen of the Jury, I felt that the miserable people had no chance of being delivered, unless the Lord would awaken his congregation and send them forth on errands of salvation. I prayed for the spirit of a Paul to lead the congregation forth upon this errand of good. I prayed for the spirit of a Loyola, to bind them in a harmony of exertion. I prayed for the spirit of a Luther to make them fearless of infringing established things, that a reformation might come about, which would need not to be reformed. I resolved to make a humble endeavour to revive again in this land the junction of manhood with religion, to add to the piety and humility of the church her ancient fearlessness and heroism.

" I do not hesitate, Gentlemen, to confess, that in this essay in the cause of Christ, I felt like the knight that breaks his first lance in the cause of honour. For the sake of Him whom I heartily serve, I have encountered all risks, albeit in an unwonted costume, and very ungainly style.

"And now, Gentlemen, let me claim your willing ear while I detail to you a little more particularly my humble services in this great cause. It appeared to me that questions touching the truths of revelation had been too long treated in a logical or scholastic method, which doth address itself to I know not what fraction of the mind ; and not finding this used in Scripture, or successful in practice, I was resolved to try another method, and appeal our cause to every sympathy of the soul which it doth naturally bear upon. We resolved to speak according as it suited the topics in hand, to the parts of human nature which the poet addresseth, to the parts of human nature which the economist addresseth, no less than to those to which the logician addresseth. Nevertheless, after a logical method, I have done so: that is, I have presented the question before these affections of the mind, in a fair and undisguised form, without fear and without partiality. In order to have a chance of a hearing, I have refrained from systematic forms of speech, and endeavoured to speak of each subject in terms proper to it, and to address each feeling in language that seemed most likely to move. I wished to argue like a man not a theologian, like a Christian not a churchman. It is these peculiarities, Gentlemen, which constituted my two new methods of handling religious truth—*the oration* and *the argument.*

" You have been told indeed by one of the witnesses to-day, whose emptiness and self-sufficiency you must have daily appreciated, that my orations and arguments differ only from sermons in the name. My orations, Gentlemen, are as purely orations or addresses to move and persuade men upon a particular point, as any of the ancient or modern models. It would have been absurd, totally absurd, to have given them any other name.

In the like manner, if the argument be not a regularly constructed argument, let its irregularities and defective parts be pointed out ; but merely to object that it shall not be so named, is nothing but another evidence of the poverty-struck invention of this age in things religious, and its resolution to remain for ever in its miserable state. The world, the thirsty spirit of the world, will never be refreshed, until more various vessels for containing and serving out the waters of life be discovered and made use of.

" The subject which I have had to agitate is the whole matter of human responsibility and future judgment, as they are set forth in the Scriptures of the Old and New Testament. My instruction, or brief, to speak technically, was taken from the revelation of God. We held no question upon the authenticity of the revelation, which we took altogether for granted. We had to do with its matter only, so that our business was not with the believer or unbeliever, but with *the man.*

" I seem to myself, allowing for occasional digression, to have kept with sufficient constancy to my subject, and generally within the sight and experience of common minds. All abstract discourse upon the responsibility in general, and the freedom and necessity of the human will, I have avoided ; not out of terror of that *marlstroom* in the ocean of thought, but because it was too nice a question to be handled by the way. Instead of such metaphysical discourse, I inquired how the nature of man accorded practically with a state of responsibility; and discovered, that in no one of its relationships was it devoid thereof, but acceded to it with a constant choice, as the very buckler of its social existence. I next passed on to peruse and consider the constitution of law and government which God hath in his mercy granted to us to live under. Here there opened upon us a wide field of ethical and political discourse. The largeness of divine law, compassing every province of purity, came under our review; the immeasurable requirements of Christ's discipline, the unanswerable demands of his judgment, the inquisition of conscience with the purer inquisition of God— these, considering well, our mind was staggered not a little, and we applied ourselves to discover the profitableness and the fitness of an institution so incommensurate with the limited powers of man—which application it pleased the Lord to reward to the satisfaction of ourselves, and we hope the profiting of others.

" Being satisfied upon the great purchase (as with a lever) which such a spiritual institution takes upon the spirit of man, to raise it to dignity and honour, we then gave ourselves to canvass the provision which it makes for our deficiencies, and to sound this question to the very bottom. Thereto we made trial of various suggestions which nature presenteth from her own stores, and which men are wont to uphold as a sufficient account of the matter. These having tried upon principles of law, and exhibited their total inadequacy to any end, except to the end of making law and responsibility altogether void, we came to the great disclosure of Christ sacrificed for the sins of men. And here we wandered, well pleased, in a glorious field. We shewed how this revelation of the gospel of peace took a pleasant powerful hold upon all our affections and all our interests, sustaining and promoting all the enthusiasm which the pure law had awakened, how it fed the lamp of knowledge with oil from heaven, and enlightened the whole house, and set all useful works on foot; how it awakened! how it cheered! how it pressed us forward!

" Ah! Gentlemen, it is sweet to speculate upon themes glorious like these. Gladly would I renew all that hath been done for the mere pleasure sake, but that the occupations of life are so many.

" Feeling within our souls an enthusiasm arise for God, we did invoke, as Elijah did of old, all the priests of Baal to the contest, and call upon them to kindle such a flame in the cold bosom of man, such an enthusiasm after holiness as this which glowed beneath the feeding hand of God, which invocation of the Anti-Christian people I again repeat, praying them right early to lay down within compass their scheme for raising fallen man, and making him great and good, and I pledge myself to give it the same impartial trial of reason and understanding which I have given unto the gospel scheme.

" We deemed it expedient to indulge our humour another turn, and for the purpose of bestirring the God-forgetting spirit of this age's policy, we adventured into the thorny path of man's political well-being, and endeavoured to study how this constitution of the gospel tended to the remedy of its ills; and here as before we reaped the fruit of our labours, finding it to be the *long sought* remedy of personal and political disorders, regenerating the sluggish and taming the fiery, and setting every subject of the realm into the position which is most easy to a good governor, and most terrible to a bad one; all which we proved by the induction of many cases, and by the ineffectual struggles which have been made and are making at social improvement, without this necessary implement of religion.

" Oh! in this crisis of the world, when thrones are shaken, and nations are arising to the work of terrible revenge, and all things are unsettled. Oh! thou Almighty Ruler of the destinies of men, make the voice of truth to be heard by the raging people, and guide them into those measures which will ensure their success, and make thy name glorious over the slavery and idolatry in which the nations are held.

" Having thus, Gentlemen, justified the constitution to which God hath made man responsible both as to its necessity, its wisdom, and its good effects, we then felt ourselves at liberty to launch upon the great question of the Future Judgment, yet cautiously and thoughtfully as one who had the conviction of wakeful reason to win; therefore we held a parley upon preliminaries, and gave her a fair field of objections, and fair liberty to complain.—We took her doubts, her rights, her very prejudices into account, to allay which, we had to entertain large discussion upon many profound questions, over which, some may think a shadow of indistinctness was notwithstanding left.

" I will own to you, Gentlemen, that here I did begin to feel the limitation of my powers. I had to forsake the realms of light, and carry the vision of my mind into the obscure of the middle state; I felt a light and a shadow upon my thoughts; they stood not constantly, but they came by glimpses, and often when I sought to write them down, they were gone.— Some apology for the cloudy indistinctness of these preliminary thoughts of judgment may be found in the active bustling spirit of this age, and especially of this, my profession, of which every individual is in some measure the slave, and of which slavery, I feel too much the influence.—This life of ours, Gentlemen, I feel to be neither an apostolic, nor a philosophic life.—It hath in it no quietness, no retirement, no contemplation. It is driven on by duty. —The spear of engagement ever galleth it.—There is no free bounding of the mind along the high courses of thought, and a narrow style of opinions hath set in upon free thought, like a stream confined within bounds, which teareth up and delugeth all the open plain. And a hot zeal for orthodoxy, consumeth speculation up, or fretteth it into madness; and the canker hath eaten so deep into the judgments of men, that I question whether any one will regard these lamentations in any better light than the murmurs of a discontented, or the reveries of an unintelligible mind.

"Whether, if thinking men should ever again be conditioned as the ancient sages were, meditating and musing like Pythagoras in the deep groves of Crotona, or like Plato, sending from the sacred promontory of Sunium his speculations abroad into boundless regions, they might not by the new aids of revelation, bring forth out of these unseen dwellings of the disembodied spirit, some light of certain understanding I do not know. But of this, I am certain, that while they live, and act, under ten thousand invasions, or their attention buried in sensual gratifications, or floating amongst ambitious vanities, and courting earthly distinctions, seeking chariots and horses, and costly abodes, and delicious entertainments, it is vain to think that either poet, or philosopher, or divine, will make any invasion upon these unredeemed provinces of thought, or even follow the flights which the more pure and self-denied spirits of former ages have taken.

"One man there is in these realms, who hath addressed himself to such a godlike life, and dwells alone amidst the grand and lovely scenes of nature, and the deep unfathomable secrecies of human thought. Would to Heaven it were allowed to others to do likewise! And he hath been rewarded with many new cogitations of nature and of nature's God, and he hath heard in

the stillness of his retreat, many new voices of his
conscious spirit, all which he hath sung in har-
monious numbers. But mark, Gentlemen, the
Epicurean soul of this degraded age! They have
frowned on him; they have spit on him; they
have grossly abused him. The masters of this
critical generation, (like generation! like masters!)
have raised the hue and cry against him, as they
have now done against me : the literary and sentimental world, which is their sounding board, hath
reverberated it; and every reptile, who can re-
tail an opinion in print, hath spread it, and given
his reputation a shock, from which it is slowly
recovering. All for what? For making nature
and his own bosom his home, and daring to sing
of the simple but sublime truths, which were revealed to him ; for daring to be free in his manner of uttering genuine feeling and depicting natural beauty, and grafting thereon, devout and
solemn contemplations of God. Had he sent his
Cottage Wanderer forth upon an excursion
amongst courts and palaces, battle fields and
scenes of faithless gallantry, his musings would
have been more welcome, being far deeper and ten-
derer, than those of the ' Heartless Child,' but
because the man hath valued virtue, and retiring
modesty, and common household truth, (as I do)
over these the ephemeral decorations or excessive
depravities of our condition, therefore is he
hated and abused.

"But, to return, Gentlemen, from this digression
—I proceeded to treat of the final adjudication to

men; of their proper allotments of praise and blame, reward and punishment. The principle of judgment being developed, we then passed on to apply it to various conditions of men, that we might shew how simple and efficient it is for the intended purpose. Here our subject properly concluded; but I thought it good to advert to two prejudices, one existing within, the other existing without the church. The former presumes that orthodox faith, the latter that our worldly accomplishments, will carry a certain weight. We demonstrated that the one view was narrow, the other erroneous.

"Having thus, Gentlemen, opened up, applied, and justified the tests of acquittal and condemnation, we were in a state to pass on to the decrees of judgment. In treating which, I endeavoured to keep from a coarse, vulgar sensuality on the one hand, and a weak, refined sentiment on the other; giving to heaven and hell some intelligible form, and some identity with the present good and bad of human conditions. For almost all Christians, in their eagerness to keep the spirit of our faith free from heathen and Mahomedan superstitions, have set forth nothing tangible upon the subject of future conditions. Their heaven is the heaven of a metaphysician or a devotee,—not of a man; their hell a bugbear only to children. In my endeavour to give breadth of exposition to this subject, I kept as close as possible to the revelation, and sought merely to become its interpreter. Having drawn our sketches to the best of our abi-

lity, we then went at length into the question of
their duration, resting it upon positive revelation,
— upon the advantages of the Christian system,—
upon the nature of God, and the nature of sin,
as known from experience; and with this ended
our argument of judgment to come, of which we
came then to exhibit the conclusion.

· " But whereas it might fare to some of my
hearers and readers to be excited by these terrible
pictures which I was fain to draw, and to cry out,
' What shall I do to be saved?' I thought it
would not be amiss to interpose an inquiry upon
the way of escape from the wrath to come. Here
I felt it needful to shake nature again out of her
insecure refuges, before opening up the only city
of refuge that holds good against the terrible day
of the Lord,—which is a life devoted to holiness,
a new birth, and a spiritual life. Here I felt tram-
meled and confined by crude and insufficient no-
tions popular in the churches; but I flinched not
from the utterance of the truth, as I believe it for
the salvation of souls. Not, Gentlemen, that I
desired to provoke controversy, but that I love
truth, and wish to see the confused mind of the
people set to rights, upon the true source and ori-
gin of the spiritual life.

" Gentlemen of the Jury, having thus joined
in harmony the word and the Spirit of God, I felt
at liberty to wind up and conclude the whole. I
cast myself as it were, sword in hand, on the
strengths in which nature shuts herself up against
all access of the thoughts of death, judgment, and

eternity. The first strong hold I encountered, was called Procrastination—but I thought it best to hold a parley with the garrison before I offered to storm the place ; I laid before them the folly of a protracted resistance ; shewed them how their commander, Postponement, was but a kidnapper of souls, and recruiting officer of Hell. I explained to them how they were living upon time as the sloth does upon the tree, till every particle of the food is consumed, then droppeth she knoweth not whither. Overcome by my arguments the garrison abandoned the place, but cast themselves into another strong hold called Bravery. I followed close upon their heels, and when I reached the fort, I meditated no parley, no tedious operation of argument, but a main attack, a storm, where the battle should be fought hand to hand, without any reserve or any mercy upon either side. They must be desperadoes, I concluded, with whom I have to deal, since our former mild and reasoning method of discourse has failed to move them. And so I set myself in the strength of God, to fight his battle with the ungodly generation. Oh ! these topers, these gamesters, these idle revellers, these hardened death despisers, these swaggering braggadocios—how they quaked for very fear in the hour of assault ; how their chivalry was made to skip, how they turned their backs, and bowed their necks, and supplicated for mercy ! After capturing Fort Bravery, there but remained the Hospital of Incurables in the hands of the enemy. You are aware, Gentlemen, that in many cases a man withereth like a tree, and in his old age is desolate of thought ; he is not pregnant with feeling, words kindle no fire in him, thoughts awake no kindred thoughts. He is of the order of incurables, whose case is perhaps the most pitiable of all. You cannot raise a spark of conviction, or kindle towards the Deity one flash of love. The whole faculties are occupied, and the old possessors will not give place ; old habits will not be disturbed ; the conscience is seared as with a red-hot iron. You would speak to him, but you know not how to begin. You do speak, and you find him intrenched in his decencies, his moralities, his charities. You cannot blast his hopes, though you know them to be hopeless, for there remaineth no chance of conviction. It would only be vexing him in vain—adding inward tribulation to outward trouble. Every thing was against interference, and the Hospital of Incurables I have therefore left in the possession of its miserable inmates, till the dread sentence is passed, when the bottomless pit shall open its mouth to receive them.

"Gentlemen of the Jury, I am now about drawing to a close what I proposed to myself to address to you. After the melancholy yet faithful picture which I have presented to your minds of the condition into which mankind are sunk ; after the simple recapitulation you have heard of the steps I have taken to rouse them from their slumbers, and of the indisputable success which has attended my endeavours, feeble though they have

M

been, I look with confidence to obtaining at your
hands a full and honourable acquittal from the various charges, some serious enough, and some contemptible enough, which have been now brought
against me. For such as refer to matters with
which the freedom of the will has nothing to do,
I nothing care, nor as it seemeth to me, are they
matters for human judgment ; yet I do confess
that it hath grieved me much that I should be
so pertinaciously charged with speaking calumni-
ously and uncharitably of my fellow men, and
of being thereto urged by the most paltry of mo-
tives, vanity, ambition, conceit, self-interest. God
doth know I would not misrepresent my fellow-
creatures whom his hand hath formed in a common mould, or rudely discover the nakedness of
their condition ; but it does irk the heart to con-
template the deep beds of degradation into which
the masses and multitudes of mankind are forced
for want of the discipline which might be wrought
on the heart by the Divine constitution, which
alone availeth to produce virtue, magnanimity,
peace, and all the finer fruits and conditions of
the soul. I know not what fearful misgivings
upon the vanity of human nature come over my
mind, when I behold the condition of unregene-
rate men, while I feel assured that there is in
the religion of Christ a power and facility to raise
them to the highest attainments of reflective and
hopeful creatures. I feel as if the better part of
man were writhing like the camp of Israel, when
bitten with fiery spirits under a deforming deadly

disease, for which the specific a thousand times approved was brought before them to their very hand, but through obstinacy, through a very love of misery and death, the infatuated people perished from present happiness and future hope. In this my sincere, honest, and zealous effort to prevent my beloved countrymen from sharing the same fate, I have besought the guidance of the Almighty and his blessing very often. 'And do thou, great source of all intelligence, forgive the errors and imperfections which thine omniscient eye beholdeth in my humble endeavours, to promote thy glory and the eternal welfare of men, remembering the limited faculties of every creature, and the clouds which sin hath induced upon the mind of man. If aught hath been uttered injurious to thy Majesty, of which thou art very jealous, do thou forgive that greatest of transgressions. If aught hath been said opposed to thy revealed word, hinder it from its evil influence upon the mind of men. As for men themselves—for my accusers—for the witnesses against me—for you Gentlemen of the Jury, who are my judges—for you noble, honourable, and venerable men, who preside over this tribunal—for all who hear me, of you I have nothing to beseech, but that you will look to yourselves, and have mercy on your own souls.'"

The effect which the reverend Defendant's address left on the audience, was marked by a deep silence for several minutes; some of the fair listeners in the gallery seemed much affected.

Mr. Phillips then rose.—He observed, that after the eloquent, convincing, triumphant, defence which the Court had just heard from his Rev. Friend, it might be deemed a matter of supererogation to bring any thing forward in the way of evidence to rebut the case for the prosecution. Just to show, however, how partially the witnesses in support of it had been selected; and how diametrically opposite their opinions were to those of men, in every respect as capable of forming a correct judgment of the merits of the Defendant, he would very briefly examine a few of the cloud of witnesses who were in waiting to give evidence in his behalf.

Editor of the London Christian Instructor and Congregational Magazine, called and examined.

Differs from Mr. Irving in matters of taste, and cannot always assent to his modes of statement, but admires his abilities, and is convinced of his ardent anxiety to do good. Conceives that Mr. Irving leaves no room for hesitation respecting either his intentions or his powers; and that he assails the conscience and the understanding in a strain of eloquent and urgent expostulation, that cannot but have with the divine blessing, a beneficial influence. His compositions are possessed neither of the depth nor elaboration of Burke, but more intense, and more effective in producing conviction. Some of his passages remind one of the march and rhythm of Milton's English prose. No imitator, he stands on his own merits—might, if he chose, take his stand, if not among the highest, at least not far below the highest of contemporary orators.

Cross-examined by Mr. Parsons.

Do you think that any advantage is gained in pulpit oratory by the adoption of antiquated forms of expression, or by the introduction of words and phrases commonly used in a low or ludicrous sense?

None. But I have no relish for the work of carping at minor defects amid substantial excellence.

Do you think that Mr. Irving's *Orations* for the Oracles of God deserve that name?

No. I will not say that they do. I perceive in them no dissimilarity from the sermon, except in a less decided use of subdivision, division, or arrangement, which is in reality the same thing and must exist in every intelligible address ; but if it be meant merely to exclude the formality of " heads," principal and subordinate, there is no novelty in the practice : it has been done by Bossuet, Chalmers, Robert Hall ; it has been expressly recommended by Cheminais, and is frequently acted upon by preachers both in and out of the establishment.

Editor of the Christian's Pocket Magazine and Anti-Sceptic examined.

Considers Mr. Irving as no inferior man. Has heard him charged as deficient in Evangelical sentiment, but denies it. Thinks that he has many admirable qualities. His language often obsolete and uncouth, with a strange mixture of that which is inflated : but it has a strength and an originality which call forth admiration. His thoughts too are novel, and his arguments have power. Believes that Providence has raised up Mr. I. for much good—Has read his book, and blushes for the boldness of those who have levelled such ungrounded charges against an estimable minister. Admires him as a man endowed with the spirit of Elijah—Has read passages of his more pointed than ever were delivered by the undaunted Knox, and not less bold—No mimic of Dr. Chalmers—Resembles him about as much as a lily resembles a rose ; the resemblance consisting in both shedding an agreeable fragrance around, and both being flowers.

Editor of the New Times, examined.

Can you tell us any thing of the Editor of the Old Times ?

A great deal. The stupid editor of that stupid paper is, as all the world well knows, a disappointed and neglected author, and equally disappointed and neglected aspirant after several other professions. His volumes are ticketted on every stall " 6d. each." He is now driven to write in the Old Times for the pot-houses.

Then you would not, perhaps, be surprised at his casting an eye of malicious envy at any successful literary character whose works might penetrate into the drawing-rooms from which his own are excluded ?

Just what I should expect, as a matter of course.

Have you read what this distempered Censor has said of the Rev. Defendant in this case?

I have; and could not help smiling at the excessive conceit which could embolden such a scribbler to assume so exalted a tone of contempt towards a man honoured by the attention of My Lords Liverpool and Stowell, Mr. Canning, Sir James Mackintosh, Mr. Peel, Mr. Brougham, and a long list of other gentlemen, the most distinguished in every department of the State.

Has himself read Mr. Irving's Orations and Arguments. Found him to be a writer of very extraordinary endowments, who has drawn largely from the stores of the Church of England, and is glad to own his obligations, as a Christian Teacher, to such men as Hooker and Taylor. His reason for not teaching to the poor exclusively, explained satisfactorily. Witness read in support of this a long extract from Burke. Thinks the Orations highly wrought. Mr. Irving employs the same weapons of animated diction and vivid imagination as his antagonists, not declining the edge of sarcasm, but turning it aside with weapons equally sharp, and opposing to the popular sophisms and errors of the day, the testimonies of conscience.—Knows that he has been called a declamatory, turgid, bombastic, writer, but has not been able to observe any of these characteristics. Considers his thoughts as clear and cogent; his expressions plain, happy, and appropriate. Eloquence, often truly striking and majestic—Conception, super-human; thoughts, overpowering; sentiments, such as " make the sealed heart knock at the ribs." Likes him the better for the roughness of antiquity which there is about him. Regards him altogether with unfeigned admiration.

Editor of the Sunday Monitor, examined.

(By the powers !) Considers Mr. Irving's popularity richly deserved. His discourses are soul-awakening. Heard him often ; and not, he trusts, without benefit. Witnessed also, with pleasure, the effect they appeared to have on the congregations assembled. Popular through the mere force of his genius, and unaided by patronage. Has created a sensation in the political, literary, and fashionable world unequalled in this country. Princes and nobles, orators and statesmen, poets and wits, beauty and fashion, have been attracted by his eloquence, as by a magnet ; and what Curran said of the celebrated Dean Kirwan, that " he came to interrupt the repose of one world, with the thunder of another," may be applied to Mr. Irving.

Cross-examined by MR. PARSONS.

You have of course observed what Mr. Irving says in his Preface, of the want of books fit for the instruction, amusement, and guide of Christians. What think you of that?

I confess that it is a proof either of ignorance or vanity.

Do you approve of his forming his style on that of the age of the Reformers ?

Not entirely. The expressions he uses are sometimes quaint and obsolete, and the sense of many passages is obscured by the " rich wardrobe of words." It is, however, the style of holy writ ; it is the phraseology of the book of Common Prayer ; it is the language of Taylor, of Bacon, of Hooker, and the venerable fathers of the church ; and as such, endeared by a thousand recollections.

Editor of the Examiner examined.

In point of doctrine, considers Mr. Irving a Calvinist ; but his claims to distinction are those of an orator and an expositionist rather than of a theologian. The theory under which Mr. Irving is seeking to appal the guilty and amaze the free, is that of bold and fearless preaching, in the style and manner of the most purely intellectual age of England. What tamed this spirit ? A political re-action, which tamed every thing English ; and this in its turn produced another, which, occurring under very different times and circumstances, has gradually made bishops just what we see them, and the church that which it is, not to mention the Kirk of Scotland, which appears, to witness, to have undergone the same happy process ; that is to say, to have been rendered very accurate in calculation, and very moderate in zeal. Holds Mr. Irving to be a sincere friend to political liberty, and that he abounds more in Christian meekness than Dr. Johnson, and less in crabstick criticism

than the Times. Speaks spiritedly and manly, in comparison
with the slaver of certain lick-spittles of the Establishment, who
are eternally prating of passive obedience, and of the piety of ex-
claiming, in the event of the existence of such a *legitimate* ruler,
Nero quand meme ! Heard Mr. Irving quote with approbation the
noble truth of the old covenanters, that " when persecution begins,
allegiance ends ;"——forcibly and honestly opposed to the non-re-
sisting cant of the clergy of the day. Until Mr. Irving is warmed
by his subject, the hearer is only struck with a full and scriptural
phraseology, in which much modern elision is rejected, some ad-
ditional conjunctions introduced, and the auxiliary verbs kept in
most active service. As he goes on, his countenance, which is
surrounded by a dark, apostolical head of hair, waving towards his
shoulders, becomes strongly expressive and lighted up, and his
gesture marked and vehement. With respect to action, has no
doubt that St. Paul at Athens has been Mr. Irving's study, a practice which is frequently diversified by an almost perpendicular ex-
tension (*see the plate, fig.* 5.) of the arm. The fabric of his orations argumentatively assertive, and his hearers not violently assailed with the peculiar dogma of Calvinism, with the exception
that Mr. Irving would by no means soften matters with respect to
hell. The grand argumentative forte of Mr. Irving consists in his
able manner of working out his great theological position,——that
revelation is necessary to men,——displays a degree of acumen and
penetration which is certainly very rare. Is a tolerable disputant,
and grants more to his sceptical disputants than most theologians.
There is a fine solemnity in his manner, but it borders on the theatrical ; the government of his vehemence, and consequently of his
voice, is sometimes out of his own management.

Cross-examined by Mr. Macvicar.

You have told us that Mr. Irving's style is formed on that of the
most purely intellectual age of England. Do you mean to say that
you approve of his assuming this antiquated garb ?
Oh, certainly not. The style is affected, the beauty indisputably
artificial. Whatever be his taste or intention in it, it is a mas-

querade habit. You have heard Mr. Irving's lamentation over poor Wordsworth? Do you think there is any foundation for it?

No. It is quite new to us that Mr. Wordsworth has been thus outrageously treated;—that some people made him a stamp distributor, we know, (similar sort of persons made Burns an exciseman)—if this be the insult alluded to, be it so; but in every other respect he has only met the common fate of all authorship. In fact, I know of no writer, in proportion to circumstances, who has received more ample homage than Wordsworth.

Do you not think that Mr. Irving at times takes a rather high ground?

Yes, frequently,—ground as visionary as Fairy land.

And is rather liberal of his attacks?

Yes, too liberal, especially against every sort of excursive and imaginative genius but his own. I could pass over what he says about his clerical brethren, but I know not on what reasonable ground the whole province of imagination is to be accommodated to the square and rule of Mr. Irving's taste and opinions. For theology has little to do in this matter. Providence, by pointing intellect to such different issues, laughs this petty assumption to scorn. Lord Byron, I suppose, is fair game, although the cant is miserable from a man of talent; but Moore receives similar condemnation, and every one who has not Mr. Irving's taste for solitude and lofty musings, which leaves nobody *living* to be praised, except himself and Mr. Wordsworth. This is puerile.

Resident Director of the Liberal examined.

[Holding, like most of the other witnesses, a mask to his face, but in so careless and shifting a manner, that any one could tell the " New Pygmalion" was behind it.]

Thinks, that the Scotch bear at present the belle, and have " got the start of the majestic world." They boast of the greatest novelists, the greatest preachers, the greatest philanthropists, and the greatest blackguards in the world. Sir Walter Scott stands at the head of them for Scotch humour, Dr. Chalmers for Scotch logic, Mr. Owen for Scotch utopianism, and Mr. Blackwood for Scotch impudence: Unrivalled four! And here is Mr. Irving, who threatens to make a fifth, and *stultify* all our London orators

N

from " kingly Kensington to Blackwall ! " Mr. Irving is the *most accomplished barbarian,* and the least offensive and most dashing clerical holder forth, the witness remembers to have seen. Puts him in mind of the first man, Adam, if Adam had but been a Scotchman, and had had coal-black hair. He seems to stand upon the integrity of his composition, to begin a new race of practising believers, to give a new impulse to the Christian religion, to regenerate the fallen and degenerate race of men. One would say, at the first glance at him, without knowing his calling or his ghostly parts, " That is the man for a fair saint." You'd swear it by

> " His foot mercurial, his martial thigh,
> The brawns of Hercules, but his jovial face ! "

Aye, there you'd stop, like Imogene—there is a want of expression in it—" The iron has not entered his soul." He has not dared to feel, but in trammels and in dread ; pleasure, fancy, and humanity, are syrens that he repels and keeps at arm's length ; and hence his features are hardened and have a barbaric crust upon them. They are not steeped in the expression of Titian or Raphael, but they would do for Spagnoletti to paint ; and his dark profile and matted locks have something of the grave commanding appearance of Leonardo da Vinci's massive portraits. Thinks Mr. Irving's voice flowery and silvery ; that he is a more amiable moralist, and more practical reasoner, than Dr. Chalmers. He throws a glancing, pleasing light, over the gloomy ground of Calvinism. There is something humane in his appeals, striking in his apostrophes, graceful in his action, soothing in the tones of his voice ; not at all affected or theatrical ; above common-place both in fancy and argument, yet hardly to be ranked as a poet or a philosopher. He is a modernized covenanter, a sceptical fanatic. His pulpit style has a resemblance to the florid gothic. It is, on the whole, polished and ambitious. Can conceive of a deeper strain of argument, of a more powerful and overwhelming flood of eloquence ; but altogether, deems him an able and attractive expounder of holy writ, and farther believes him to be an honest man.

Cross-examined by MR. MACVICAR.

Is the account you have given to-day of Mr. Irving the same which you gave to the readers of the Liberal, some weeks ago ?

I have said nothing to-day, Sir, but what I have said before in that publication.

Perhaps less, Sir. You have told us to-day, that there is something very " *humane*" and *soothing* in Mr. Irving's appeals.——Did you not say, at the same time, in the Liberal, that there was something very *exclusive* and *intolerant* in his plan of exalting Religion as the *thaumaturgos*, or wonder-worker in the reform of mankind, reconcileable neither to sound reason, nor to history.

Yes; I do remember saying something of that sort.

You have told us also to-day, that you believe Mr. I. " to be *an honest man ?*" Did you not add in the Liberal, that " you did *not feel exactly on sure grounds with him,*—that *you scarcely knew whether he preaches Christ crucified, or himself ?*"

Yes.

And in illustration of that, you took notice of certain liberties with the divine character, in which Mr. I. is apt to indulge ?

I did: for example, his talking of *Jesus Christ destroying melody;*" and the " *Mouth of God being muzzled by man.*" Nor did I hesitate to censure these expressions as contrary to every allowed licence of speech.

Could these expressions have been slips of the tongue ?

Not likely; for Mr. Irving preaches from written notes, and his printed volume contains, I am told, expressions which are a great deal worse.

The Chief Justice, observing that Mr. Phillips was about to call another witness, recommended to him to consider whether he was exercising a sound discretion, in the line of examination he was pursuing.

MR. PHILLIPS.——Some of my witnesses, it is true, have broken down rather unexpectedly. I will venture, however, one more.

Editor of the Museum examined.

Considers Mr. Irving's volume of Pulpit Eloquence, a work of a most unusual and interesting character; the production of no ordinary mind; the fruit of no common soil or every day culture. Occasionally we have all the tenderness of Massilon, now and then the fire and impetuosity of Bourdaloue; at other times the picturesque vigour and raciness of Crabbe. Could point to passages, which in felicity of imagery and harmony of style, are not exceeded by any thing in the whole compass of the English language. Conceives the most prominent feature of Mr. Irving's style to be a certain tone of soothing tenderness, a love of mankind in the humbler departments of life. Exhorting, encouraging, entreating them to know their stake in the great interests of this world, and in the contemplation of their heavenly Redeemer. Yet is free to confess, that Mr. Irving's metaphors are so frequent, so bold, and sometimes so lengthened and spun out, that we become weary of comprehending them.—His pages are not " milk for babes," but strong meat for strong men.—Hardly knows any volume, which is, upon the whole, likely to reflect more substantial credit upon its author, or to produce more salutary effects to the body politic. Wishes it to be attentively perused by *all* classes of society, under the conviction that it will do much to promote the best interests of social order and vital religion.

Cross-examined by MR. PARSONS.

Of what creed of faith do you hold Mr. Irving to be ?
I am delighted, Sir, to perceive that he is *no Calvinist.*
Of what creed is the Scottish Church ?
Calvinistic.
Does Mr. Irving belong to that Church ?
He does.
And must have signed its articles ?
Of course.
Admirable witness ! to be delighted that the object of his praise does not believe the faith which he has subscribed and sworn to maintain.

Mr. Phillips declined calling any more wit-nesses.

Mr. Sergeant Bishop waived his right of reply; and in doing so, could not omit tendering his grateful thanks to his learned friend, Mr. P. for the great pains he had taken, during the preceding hour, to render all reply unnecessary.

The Chief Justice charged the Jury in his usual plain, and perspicuous manner. He described the case to the jury as one of unprecedented import-ance. Well might the Reverend Defendant tell them all to look to their own souls; for the ques-tion at issue was, neither more nor less, than whe-ther they were not one and all in the broad road to perdition, notwithstanding the many thousand guides whom they employed and paid well to prevent them from straying from the right path. The jury were in fact sitting in judgment on the whole clergy of the united empire; for if the Rev. Defendant were really no mere pretender, as he is charged to be—if one half of all he says be true, then are all the rest of his clerical brethren (with such ex-ceptions only as Mr. I. may be pleased to point out) a set of the most unfaithful stewards that ever lived. In proportion to the magnitude of these pretensions was, however, the difficulty of coming to the consideration of them, with minds as free and unbiassed as they ought to be. We were apt to start back from the claim of any man to be so much better and more enlightened than his fellows, and without admitting for a moment

the possibility of the thing, were very likely to
set him down at once, as that quack and brawler
which Mr. I. was here alleged to be. When he
looked, however, to the high respectability, intelligence and discrimination of the gentlemen he
addressed, he felt confident, that from their minds
every prejudice of this kind must have been dis-
missed, and that they had come to this enquiry,
as open to a conviction that the clergy deserve
all the opprobrium heaped upon them, as that Mr.
Irving is entitled to the extraordinary precedence
which he demands. The indictment, he was sorry
to observe, was every carelessly and loosely drawn.
The first count touching the defendant's personal
appearance, could not go to the jury at all. It
was not laid on any rule of common sense ; no
punishment could possibly follow a conviction
upon it. If a charge lay anywhere on this score,
it was against nature, for casting so intellectually-
gifted a gentleman as Mr. I. in so coarse a cor-
poreal mould. Neither could the sixth count,
which imputed to Mr. I, a commonness of understanding, as a fault, be at all entertained ; he liked
men of common understanding, and only wished
we had more of them ; it was by pretending to a
more than a common share that there were so many
knaves and dupes in the world. The remaining
five counts certainly contained fair enough matters for human judgment, and these he would
send to the jury. At the same time it was
easy to perceive from the loose manner in which

they were worded, from the width of the meshes
of which the net was constructed, that they
might, after all, catch nothing. The REV ED-
WARD IRVING might be a Mr. Merryman, but
he would at all events be no merry-*Andrew*; he
might be a quack, but no " *common*" one ; a
brawler, but no " *common*" one ; a swearer, but
no " *common*" one. Now, if the jury thought that
in any one of these respects the defendant was
something more than common, they could not,
though thus superlatively guilty, convict him on
this indictment, but must give him the benefit of
their verdict. The seventh and last count seemed
to be the only one drawn up with any distinctness
and comprehensiveness ; and perhaps the jury
would direct their chief attention to the bearing
of the evidence upon it. Much he wished to
have been able to assist them by a digest of
that evidence ; but the task was one from which
he shrunk in dismay. It was obviously a matter
of no ordinary nicety and difficulty to balance
such a mass of conflicting authorities, to say how
much one was entitled to respect, and how little
another. It might be a perilous thing too, to say
all one thought of such and such—their corrupt
leanings, their base subserviency, their low abuse,
their habitual lying, their matter-of-business,
praise, and censure. He preferred, on all these
accounts, leaving the Jury to judge for themselves on which side the evidence preponderated,
not doubting that they would bring in such a verdict as would fully meet the justice of the case.

The Jury then retired, and after the lapse of about an hour, the Jury returned into court.

Foreman. "We find the defendant guilty on the seventh count of the indictment—not guilty on all the others. I am desired, however, by my brother Jurymen, to state, that but for the manner in which several of the counts are laid, as remarked on by your Lordship, our verdict would have been very different.

The defendant was ordered to be brought up for judgment next term; but it is understood that he intends to move for a new trial.

THE END.

LONDON:

SHACKELL AND ARROWSMITH, JOHNSON'S-COURT, FLEET-STREET.